AMERICA-LITE

America-Lite

HOW IMPERIAL ACADEMIA
DISMANTLED OUR CULTURE
(and Ushered In the Obamacrats)

David Gelernter

Encounter Books  New York • London

First American edition published in 2012 by Encounter Books,
an activity of Encounter for Culture and Education, Inc.,
a nonprofit, tax exempt corporation.
Encounter Books website address: www.encounterbooks.com

Manufactured in the United States and printed on
acid-free paper. The paper used in this publication meets
the minimum requirements of ANSI/NISO Z39.48 1992
(R 1997) (*Permanence of Paper*).

FIRST AMERICAN EDITION

LIBRARY OF CONGRESS CATALOGING-IN-PUBLICATION DATA
Gelernter, David.
America-lite: how imperial academia dismantled our culture
(and ushered in the obamacrats)/David Gelernter.
p. cm.
Includes bibliographical references and index.
ISBN 978-1-59403-606-4 (hardcover: alk. paper)
1. United States—Intellectual life—20th century. 2. Education, Higher—Political
aspects—United States—History—20th century. 3. United States—Social
conditions—1945– 4. Social change—United States—History—20th century.
5. Political culture—United States—History—21st century. I. Title.
E169.12.G45 2012
973.91—dc23
2012003170

For my Jane, my mother and my father

Contents

Acknowledgments

MANY THANKS TO GLEN LOWRY AND LYNN CHU FOR HELPING TO INVENT THIS book, and to Encounter Books and especially Roger Kimball for being patient and accommodating far above and beyond the call of duty. Thanks most of all to my brilliant editor Carol Staswick for pounding the manuscript into shape.

Before and After

EVERYONE KNOWS THAT AMERICAN CIVILIZATION CHANGED IN THE 1960S and '70s. When President Obama's generation reached adulthood in the 1980s and afterward, the nation had altered fundamentally from the one in which their parents grew up. A revolution in American culture had transformed the landscape. Let's take a quick tour around this cultural revolution—glance it over from outside. Then we will stop the bus and get off and look deeper.

Before the cultural revolution, it was taken for granted that instilling patriotism was a duty of every U.S. public school. After the revolution, ROTC disappeared entirely from the Ivy League, not to return until 2011.

Before the cultural revolution, America was assumed to be a Christian or Judeo-Christian society. As Britain struggled against Nazi Germany in 1940, President Roosevelt said in a radio address, "Today the whole world is divided between human slavery and human freedom—between pagan brutality and the Christian ideal."

Before the cultural revolution, police duties used to be described as protecting the citizenry from "crime and vice." "See you in church" meant "see you around." "Red-blooded American" was used routinely and without irony, as in: "Hemingway and Steinbeck are red-blooded American authors."

Before the cultural revolution, literature, music and fine arts were increasingly the property not only of the rich but of the educated middle classes. When John Kennedy invited Robert Frost to read a poem at his inauguration, Frost's poetry was known all over the English-speaking world. Frost himself was a first-rate international celebrity, along with other big-league artists. A Hemingway or Calder, a Leonard Bernstein or Copland or Picasso was respected in the art world, but all these men were top-draw celebrities also. Today, virtually no one outside the arts community knows of a living poet, painter or classical composer.

Before the cultural revolution, there was no sex education in public schools. Sex and sexuality (including homosexuality) were inappropriate topics for classroom discussion in high school, not to mention the lower grades. Before the cultural revolution, access to birth control was restricted, in theory, to married couples. The legal status of abortion was regulated separately by each state.

Before the cultural revolution, there were no coed college dormitories with young men and women living in bedrooms on the same floor. Before the cultural revolution, visiting between men and women students on campus was regulated by "parietals," which limited male visiting in female dormitories to certain times, and usually required girls to return to their dormitories by set hours and to sign out before leaving for the evening, listing their destinations or plans. When men visited women in their rooms or vice versa, the "three on the floor" rule came into play: the door must always be open and there must be three feet on the floor the whole time.

(I remember learning about parietals, when I was a young teenager, from a college student who had witnessed their abolition with satisfaction. He was a counselor at tennis camp, a type of summer camp where you did nothing but play tennis all day long, grunting occasionally as needed; no nonsense about tents or kayaks or campfires. In the late 1960s, you wore white on the courts—not pale buff, not powder blue; *white*.)

Modern commentators are apt to express routine anger that girls were regulated so much more strictly than boys. But the colleges were legally *in loco parentis,* in the parent's place, until court decisions in the 1960s and '70s freed them from this tight spot; and they set a more careful watch on girls because girls were more vulnerable than boys, more likely to be abused. Do modern liberals deny that women are more likely to be abused? They like to believe that the sexes are interchangeable. And they'd also like to believe that crimes committed by men against women are a much worse problem than crimes committed by women against men—which is only common sense. But you can't have it both ways. Are we interchangeable or not?

The destruction of the etiquette that used to govern relations between men and women, along with many other rules of the social road, is one of the deepest, darkest consequences of the revolution, and one of the least understood. Of course, custom and etiquette evolve constantly, and new customs arise to replace old ones. But it takes many years for new and natural customs to emerge. *How else but in custom and in ceremony / are innocence and beauty born?* (Yeats.)

The deliberate smashing of etiquette in the wake of America's cultural revolution—everyone please toss your ancient crystal stemware *that* way, straight into the fireplace, thank you!— reminds one of similar destructive acts early in the French and Soviet revolutions. The French quickly returned to their old ways ("think left, live right," say the French, dropping their principles in the trash on the way out), whereas post-Soviet Russia remains a lawless and dangerous society. America, on the other hand, still has two deep reservoirs of manners and etiquette: the military and some conservative churches. America is always a special case, and this story is not over yet.

What many observers fail to consider when they shrug off or laugh off the protocols that used to govern social relations, especially between men and women, is that "good manners" and "proper etiquette" are names for *formal* behavior. And everyone carries out formal rules in approximately the same way. Formal behavior is rehearsed. Informal or unmannerly behavior is improvised, unrehearsed. Because it *is* unrehearsed and improvised, it reveals personality in a way that formal behavior never can. Mannerly, formal behavior is a screen protecting from view the informal, improvised behavior that is self-revealing.

"Do not expose your private affairs, feelings or innermost thoughts in public. You are knocking down the walls of your house when you do." (Emily Post, *Etiquette*, 1940.)[1]

In assaulting the protective shell provided by etiquette or good manners, the cultural revolution and its consequences promoted the destruction of privacy; in fact, of the whole idea of privacy. The internet, too, makes it easy to party naked. The extent to which young people responded to the internet by voluntarily stripping off their privacy is startling. But it wouldn't have happened—not to the same extent—if the revolution hadn't prepared the way. Andrew Ferguson recently wrote about the mainstream press's incomprehension of Donald Rumsfeld, who was unwilling to reveal his innermost emotions in public, even while being interviewed by the highest-paid talent on television.[2] Bitter old man.

Before the cultural revolution, one's elders and those in authority were sometimes addressed as *Sir, Madam, Miss.* First names were used ordinarily by permission, among friends. College teachers called their students "Mr. Robinson," "Miss Whitney," as if they were grownups. These small touches gave society a more formal and therefore a more private tone.

Custom and ceremony, manners and etiquette are eggshells easily crushed, impossible to reassemble. The etiquette between teachers and students that made colleges function socially and not just intellectually, and—vastly more important—the customs that governed relations between women and men (or rather, ladies and gentlemen) were largely destroyed. It was easy for feminists to order men to stop treating women like ladies: taking off hats, rising, holding doors, leading the way downstairs and following upstairs, paying a lady's way when you have asked her out, and so on. Men were only too happy to oblige. Men never were big etiquette enthusiasts.

But it turned out that this sort of etiquette was the rubric under which nearly all other sorts were organized. The sledgehammering of the ideas of "lady" and "gentleman" led to the destruction of good manners generally. And feminists, despite their terrible strength and Achillean wrath, would have been unable—had they tried—to invent and impose a new etiquette to replace the old. A new crop of manners must be patiently awaited. Such crops mature slowly, over generations.

One change is harder to see and measure than any other; it can only be felt. But it is the most important of all. In a previous book, *1939: The Lost World of the Fair,* I put it this way:

> Authority still lingers in small pockets here and there.
> But those are tidal pools; the grand sweep of ocean is
> far away. Power remains today just as it always has,
> but not authority. Authority has all but vanished. Its
> disappearance from American life is just as significant
> an event, I believe, as the closing of the frontier.
>
> Authority in 1939 New York was vested, of course,
> in the country's powerful and popular president. It
> was vested in Mayor LaGuardia, Parks Commissioner
> Moses, renowned pastor Dr. Harry Emerson Fosdick
> of Riverside Church, Columbia University's eminent
> president, Nicholas Murray Butler; and in teachers,
> priests, rabbis and ministers throughout the city, in
> the *Herald Tribune* and the *New York Times,* in mothers
> and in fathers. Authority was vested in the cop on the
> beat, even in the railway conductor on his rounds.[3]

The cultural revolution swept it all away.

And the most far-reaching of all revolutionary transformations: in the two decades following 1965, the proportion of young mothers who worked full-time rose from one-third to two-thirds. This colossal shift of energy and focus had deep consequences for the economy, for the rearing and education of children, and in the unease so many young parents feel so persistently. The economic consequences were large and good, although they have been insufficiently studied: breaking open a vast new keg of potential talent was steroid for American productivity. But who keeps track of the costs? Perhaps those are recorded only at the deepest levels of human personality laid down in childhood, never revealed.

So the cultural revolution's message—its doctrine, viewpoint, ideology—covers many topics, from race to religion, from attitudes about America to beliefs about the meaning of family. You may approve some or all of these changes. Whether you do or not, you cannot deny that the United States has been profoundly transformed. Before the cultural revolution, Americans lived a different kind of life, in a different texture of time.

chapter one

Intellectuals and the Cultural Revolution

IN 1957, WILLIAM DEVANE, DEAN OF YALE, MADE A CASUAL STATEMENT THAT no one noticed at the time. But in retrospect it's remarkable.

> Our national leaders for the most part are men of integrity, idealism, and skill; our literary and artistic people command an international respect such as they never had before; our scientists and engineers, especially the latter, are the wonder and envy of other nations; our teachers in our colleges and universities are learned and devoted.[1]

In 1957, Americans were pleased with America and proud of it. They had problems and knew it, but were undismayed.

Less than twenty years later, that proud confidence was gone, crumbled like mud-bricks into flyblown clouds of dust. "No one knows which way to turn and which way to go," wrote the great essayist (and lifelong optimist, patriot, liberal) E. B. White in 1975.[2] "Patriotism is unfashionable," he wrote in 1976, "having picked up the taint of chauvinism, jingoism, and demagoguery. A man is not expected to love his country, lest he make an ass of himself."[3] The nation got over its low spirits, but Americans no longer speak about their country the way DeVane did back in 1957.

The dean of Yale had spoken with comfortable pride—the relaxed, easy pride of a father whose child is a success and everyone knows it; the pride of a patriot whose country can tolerate being admired. He expressed the old elite's belief in Americanism.

Among patriotic doctrines, Americanism is nearly unique in being a whole political worldview. Its creed is liberty, equality, democracy, and American Zionism: America as the promised land, the shining city on a hill, a nation tasked by God to be a beacon to the world; to be the world's only biblical republic. Thomas Jefferson, in his second inaugural, confirmed the colonial doctrine of the New Promised Land, of America as the New Israel. "I shall need," he said, "the favor of that Being in whose hands we are, who led our fathers, as Israel of old, from their native land and planted them in a country flowing with all the necessaries and comforts of life."

America had a mission, as Abraham Lincoln said: "With malice toward none, with charity for all, with firmness in the right as God gives us to see the right, let us strive on to finish the work we are in." America is always in the midst of great work—making itself better; resolving its contradictions and problems; realizing its own nature; transforming itself step by step, inch by inch into that shining city. "The United States," said the French minister of culture and distinguished writer André Malraux, at the White House in 1962, "is the first nation to become the most powerful in the world without having sought to be so. Its exceptional energy and organization have never been oriented to conquest."[4] Auden called it, simply, "the first egalitarian society."[5]

Today, when Americans praise their own nation, they do it defiantly; that unselfconscious patriotic pleasure is gone. What caused the American mood to crumble between William DeVane's statement and E. B. White's? The civil rights struggle couldn't be the answer; for one thing, it united rather than divided the country, except for the segregationist Old South. Maybe the bitter split over the war in Vietnam explains it. But that can't be right; can't be the whole truth. Antiwar protests were powered by the New Left and "the Movement," which originated in Tom Hayden's "Port Huron Statement" of 1962, before the nation had ever heard of Vietnam. And the New Left picked up speed at Berkeley in the Free Speech Movement of 1964 and early '65, before the explosion of Vietnam. Bitterness toward America was an evil spirit shopping for a body when Vietnam started to throb during 1965.

Norman Mailer, an elder statesman or court jester of the antiwar movement, had vented his explosive, histrionic bitterness at American society back in 1956, in the "morally gruesome" (as Norman Podhoretz called it)[6] "White Negro," an essay that endorses, backhandedly, black murder and mayhem against whites.[7] Vietnam was Pandora's box in reverse, where all the restless, violent, hate-ragged rancor in America came swirling together into a cultural black hole. Not for nothing was the 1955 James Dean movie *Rebel Without a Cause* an icon for Mailer, who mentioned it in his notorious piece, and for the hipsters of the late 1950s, who flowed into the hippies and Yippies and the Movement of the 1960s. First came hatred, then the cause. But why rebel *without* one?

Of course I have already named a cause, or DeVane has: despite its struggles over integration and its Cold War fears and tensions, America was a thriving, powerful, exuberant, virile, blooming nation in the 1950s and early '60s; and young Americans—the brooding Hamlets among them—were haunted by their fathers' monumental achievement in making it so. And the sullen, swaggering Iagos felt stifled, and jealous of what their fathers had done without their help: in the Second World War, those fathers had beaten out the very fires of hell. No feat could stand beside that without seeming small, and who would ever admire them as their fathers had been admired? *O, beware, my lord, of jealousy, / It is the green-eyed monster which doth mock / The meat it feeds on.* (Iago to Othello.) But there is more to it.

To find out what, we must reach for a different time and place: Britain during the Second World War. "The sniggering of the intellectuals at patriotism . . . has done nothing but harm," wrote the great author and thinker George Orwell in 1940.[8] "In England," he wrote, "patriotism takes different forms in different classes, but it runs like a connecting thread through nearly all of them. Only the Europeanized intellectuals are really immune to it."[9]

Forward to 1975, and E. B. White again: "Patriotism is unfashionable . . . . A man is not expected to love his country."

Here is another way of measuring: In the 1950s, the proportion of American children born to unmarried mothers was stable at around 5 percent. During the '60s it started moving upward, and by 1975, when E. B. White spoke for a nation in anguish, it had reached 10 percent. And it kept rising: to 30 percent in 1995 and 41 percent today. (The 41 percent includes 73 percent of non-Hispanic black children, 53 percent of Hispanic and 29 percent of non-Hispanic whites.) This is bad news for American children, as we have known for decades. Children who grow up with a father and a mother on the premises do better in almost every way than children of single mothers. Many studies confirm the fact, which (after all) we already knew; it's only common sense.

While the count of illegitimate babies was rising like an apparition out of the desert, the eminent sociologist James Q. Wilson wrote in 1995, "There is no more radical a cultural division in all of history than that between the attachment ordinary people have for the family and the hostility intellectuals display toward it."[10]

Many people suppose that intellectuals (as Auden wrote of poets) make nothing happen. But what if they *do* make things happen? Where would that put us? Up a creek is the right answer. Patriotism has been beaten bloody and the family is on the ropes. It has been a great epoch for American intellectuals.

––•––

Intellectuals are rebels without causes. Chess players look for games and intellectuals look for arguments. They *must* champion unpopular causes, *must* oppose society or they will get no pick-up arguments—and arguing is their world; it is what they do. "Dispute was his art form," said Mary McCarthy, wistfully, about her once-lover Philip Rahv—a leading figure among midcentury New York intellectuals.[11] "He thinks too much," said Julius Caesar about Cassius; "such men are dangerous." Cassius was dangerous not because he brooded constantly but because he brooded about *himself* constantly, and about his grievances. Intellectuals do that.

Intellectuals are always a minority and, no matter how influential they become, they are always the straight man. They almost never rise to the most powerful positions in this or any society. And they make less money than people of comparable education and intelligence in other lines of work. You would have to be an out-of-work, freelance ditch digger to make less—anyway, that's how it seems to intellectuals. They are supposed to have their minds on bigger things than mere stuff got with money, and often they do; but still they have mortgages and bills to pay and children to propel (slowly and painfully) through college, dollar by dollar by dollar, with tuition and fees rising every ten seconds. For all these reasons, disaffection or "alienation" comes with the job. Of course they are rebels. Any society that does not give its intellectuals money, does not give them prestige but *does* give them cultural influence is grossly foolish; is asking for trouble. And almost deserves what it gets.

Constitutionally aggrieved as they may be, there has been a radical change in the role of American intellectuals: a cultural revolution that took place during the post–World War II generation, 1945–1970. It changed America so dramatically the change is hard to measure or grasp—like a fireworks bloom that leaves you dazed, stunned, temporarily seeing nothing but the flash itself re-echoing in strange colors; or a strong right jab to the face that yields similar results. The revolution transformed America's identity: fixed this nation up with a new life story, new worldview, new opinions. How could anyone miss a revolution—and such a big one?

Answer: the flash (culminating in the grandiose late 1960s) was dazzling, but the changes it created have been emerging gradually ever since. As in all revolutions, the struggle came first and then its consequences, which are still developing. The knockout punch is quick, but you might spend a long time on the mat. And your face might be rearranged forever.

The conventional view is that the civil rights movement and Vietnam and feminism are what changed the country. But the antiwar movement and modern feminism were *consequences* of the revolution. The civil rights movement sustained and expanded the revolution. For the thing itself, we have to look elsewhere.

The cultural revolution began right after World War II and was concluded triumphantly by around 1970. The effects of the revolution on American society were already making themselves felt in the late '60s, before the struggle was over. The first wave of consequences was complete by the late '80s. And the effects continue to take shape today. The revolution itself was made of just two big events.

First, the Great Reform of elite American colleges, which changed them from society colleges into intellectuals' colleges. The reform was a coup of the intellectuals, in which they took control of a vessel where they had previously only been passengers (and in many cases, third-class passengers). I present no list of elite colleges; the term is elastic on purpose. I'm speaking of a hundred-odd schools, give or take. I will give many examples.

The other big event, simultaneous with the Great Reform but separate from it, was the rise of Imperial Academia. Professional schools and graduate schools and the bachelor's degree itself grew steadily more important. A nation that had once prided itself on its neat display of fancy academic houseplants now found itself surrounded by them, as their outward-pushing branches and relentlessly exploring tendrils pushed into every corner of America's life. The intellectuals' college became the Imperial University. Elite universities had always been influential in American culture, but in the generation after World War II they took charge. Thereafter, American culture was in their hands, because of the enormous influence of their alumni and the direct influence of the institutions themselves—on journalism, business, the arts, every other college in the country and (most important) on grade school teaching at every level.

This changing of the palace guard, and the growing importance of the palace itself, was no mere bureaucratic shuffle. The revolution delivered a powerful message, like an explosive left hook: "Left-liberalism is good for America; left-liberalism is the standard by which all political ideas must be judged." Intellectuals tend to have strong political opinions, usually left-liberal ones. The great critic Lionel Trilling, describing the character of "the American intellectual class," calls it, "through all mutations of opinion, predominantly of the Left."[12] And the cultural revolution didn't merely launch lots of left-liberal ideas into circulation; it allowed left-libs to capture the plates and the presses and the whole cultural money supply. Thereafter, down to the present, intellectuals have controlled the standard of value in American culture.

Because they are natural rebels, intellectuals are natural left-wingers. Yet the facts are easy to misconstrue. Among intellectuals who care about politics, government and national affairs, about three-quarters (let's say) are left-liberals—an enormous majority, though it would seem to leave plenty of conservatives to go around. But in reality, conservative intellectuals are tremendously rare. The reason is a multiplier effect that's simple and important.

Politics probably matters to around 10 percent of intellectuals; the other 90 percent don't care much. Within the inner political core, three-quarters is more than enough to set the tone or drift. And the resulting impression in the institution: "the political people around here are strongly Democratic." (Turn on three heaters and one air conditioner, and the room still gets warm.) So the 90 percent of intellectuals who don't care much about politics are likely to become left-libs just to accommodate the committed kernel. And left-liberalism propagates through the intelligentsia like a ripple on a smooth lake. It leaves the committed conservative 2.5 percent unchanged, while nearly all the rest are turned various shades of left.

Add to this the undoubted talents of intellectuals and their propensity to feel distinctly superior to everyone else, plus their relatively low salaries and status (outside their own circles), and there is more than enough to account for an American intelligentsia that's 97.5 percent left-liberal, or thereabouts. It's only human nature.

———

Today, intellectuals are smothering American society. They are not doing it on purpose, not conspiring. (Do algae conspire to choke a pond?) They are just going about their business.

What is their business? What is an intellectual? "To be a littérateur," wrote the great German Jewish thinker Walter Benjamin, "is to live under the sign of mere intellect, just as prostitution is to live under the sign of mere sex."[13] Substitute *intellectual* for *littérateur* . . .

But that's not fair. We'll try again.

An intellectual is a theory maker. Intellectuals sit on their front porches cutting, sewing, patching, mending theories. An intellectual's job is to account for facts, or replace them, by theories. An intellectual substitutes for the intractable bloody mess called reality a seamless, silken tapestry of pure ideas.

All thinkers use abstraction and invent theories; inventing theories *is* thinking. But a theory must be transparent and flexible to be any good. When facts change or new facts emerge, the theory must be adjusted or, if need be, thrown out. An effective thinker cares passionately about theories and abstractions but is obsessed with reality, keeps his eye on the ball, never loses sight of the facts.

Intellectuals, however, are subject to a dangerous occupational hazard—dangerous to the rest of the world, that is. The hazard is to study theories instead of facts. Facts are messy and sticky and ugly, the half-sucked lollipops of Fate. Theories are simpler and sometimes beautiful. And so intellectuals are too likely to turn into professional Christos, hiding huge volumes of ugly reality under acres of simple pink wrapper tied with a ribbon. Intellectuals are too likely to be cognitively nearsighted: theories stay sharp while the facts behind them go all fuzzy. "It is a mistake to think that an intellectual is required to be intelligent," writes Mary McCarthy; "there are occasions when the terms seem to be almost antonyms."[14] More precisely: most intellectuals *are* intelligent, but their insistence on peering at the world through cotton-candy theories means that, smart as they might be, they are (unfortunately) predisposed to beliefs that are silly and false.

Nowadays we don't like to generalize, lest we should arrive at inconvenient or forbidden conclusions about some nation or race or religion. "But I am considering each of these groups as a whole," writes Julien Benda, the wise and cranky French Jew who called intellectuals of an earlier generation to account in his masterpiece, *Treason of the Intellectuals* (1928). "This means that I shall not feel myself contradicted by a reader . . . so long as this reader is obliged to admit that as a whole each of these groups does manifest the characteristics I have indicated."[15]

An exclusive taste for the theoretical sets an intellectual apart from other thinkers or writers or artists or scholars or scientists who are just as smart and know just as much as he does. An ordinary thinker hungers for concrete detail. He wants to get down and play in the sand, feel the grit beneath his fingernails, smell the dust, see the quartz points sparkle in the sun: wants to know all about real people and places and things and goings-on. This love of concrete detail is just as clear in Richard Feynman's classic three-volume introduction to physics (the "abstract" science of physics) as in any good novel or history book. But to an intellectual, those details are just distracting gossip and noise. The theory—the *backbone* of reality, not the trivial little fish bones that encumber it—is what's important.

A small child might invent a theory that says "a rose is a red flower." If someone shows the child-theorist a pink rose, he might say to himself, "pink is (after all) merely pale or watered-down red, so my theory is still valid." Now suppose someone shows him a white rose; he might say, "white isn't really a color at all, it's the absence of color, and this poor specimen is probably an albino or some kind of atypical exception. My theory holds."

So far, he has been acting like any effective thinker. Theories or abstractions are the way we understand the world. The real challenge comes when someone shows him a yellow rose. An effective thinker will say, "I conclude that my theory is wrong." An intellectual will say, "I conclude that this isn't a rose."

Theorizing is the reason men *understand* and don't just sit passively in the bleachers and snooze. We need theories to think; can't think without them. Yet theories can be dangerous. To reel round the world with blinders on can be deadly, to you and everyone in your path.

A simple example from the 1960s: Mainstream (left) intellectuals had a theory that all children learn better in racially integrated classrooms. In the South, the races had been separated by law, and it was fairly easy to abolish those unjust laws and allow the races to mix naturally in school. The theorizers then turned their attention elsewhere. In some northern cities, they found schools that were nearly all black. No law said they had to be, but the schools were in black neighborhoods (often slum neighborhoods) where no whites lived, and so, naturally, the schools were mainly black.

But the theory said that *schools must be racially mixed*. So the intellectuals said, "Fine; let's go find some white children and ship them in—and ship some black children out." This brilliant solution led to the idiocy of forced busing, whereby white children were loaded on buses and driven right past their own schools in their own neighborhoods deep into strange neighborhoods, where they were dumped in strange schools. Often these faraway neighborhoods were crime-ridden and dangerous, as a special bonus. At the end of the day, the children were put back on buses and hauled home. Meanwhile, black children also found themselves herded onto buses and hauled to strange neighborhoods and unfamiliar schools. It would have been more efficient if a large transport plane had simply scooped up a load of white children at a central depot every morning, and then dropped them—equipped with parachutes, of course—at all the right places. This might have been the obvious next step had the policy been allowed to mature.

Insofar as race bigotry caused those dangerous all-black neighborhoods, it was unjust that blacks should have had to live and go to school there. But the right solution could not possibly have been to import white children, because that only added a second injustice to the first. But mainstream left-intellectuals care about *Justice,* not justice; not mere human beings. "Disregard for truth and the preference for ideas over people," writes the English historian Paul Johnson, "marks the true secular intellectual."[16]

Johnson is decidedly conservative, but this view of intellectuals is hardly restricted to conservatives. George Orwell's view of intellectuals, as Trilling summarizes it, was this: "the contemporary intellectual class did not think and did not really love the truth."[17] For all Trilling's courtly restraint in restating it, this is a shocking accusation. *Intellectuals do not think.* "The most irresponsible and corrupt group of all," writes the thinker and critic Nicola Chiaromonte (about Italy in the post–World War II generation), "is, I would say unhesitatingly, today's intellectuals. They follow the crowd instead of setting an example, quibble instead of thinking . . . ."[18] Worse: they are not *really* truthful (says Orwell). They rate "true theories" higher than mere, trifling, accidental, disorganized, dirty *fact.*

Keeping political theories in tune with reality can be hard, discouraging work. The left and the right are equally apt to neglect it.

But just now it happens to be the left that is blinded by obsolete theories.

When young people learn left-liberal theories at school instead of facts, they can't *see* America no matter how hard they try. They see only the ridiculous, grotesque masks that intellectuals have fashioned: Western civilization is distinguished mainly by awfulness, likewise the United States; there is no great literature; there are no heroes (or none who are white males); Judeo-Christian religion is a curse; patriotism is absurd; there is no high culture; there are no ethical absolutes; no one has the right to be "judgmental"; and so on. Too many teachers show their students only this horrible *masked* America, because for too many teachers it is the only America they know. They were reared and educated wholly in the Masked Era.

There are two Americas, one real, one masked. The real nation is implausibly large, four hundred years deep in the tall weeds and wildflowers of time, a doer of grave wrongs and magnificent rights, complex but ultimately (beyond all question) great and beautiful. And the masked nation: much simpler, theory-shrouded, yet ominous and frightening and dangerous. President Obama calls himself "a student of history." But he studied masked America, as we will see.

The opaque, smooth, soft, silken cobweb of theory spun by intellectuals reflects a deliberate choice. The intelligentsia has repeatedly *chosen* not to know mere, concrete, gritty facts. It has chosen to be ignorant of what is actually happening in the world, by picking its facts and news sources to avoid the slightest upset to elegant finished theories or tender and perhaps underdeveloped intellectual organs. Silken shrouds that hide messy details and sharp edges, and make big pictures invisible, are valuable to intellectuals and (so they believe) to their students. An intellectual who teaches at a top college will have students who land fancy, influential jobs, and the ed school that is part of the university learns to teach masked history too, so it will be passed on faithfully.

Intellectuals invent theories and teach them to Airheads. Airheads learn them and believe them. In an intellectual's classroom, some students become disciples—intellectuals in their own right. Some reject the whole nonsense and become realists. The vast middle group, Airheads-to-be, simply sunbathe and, without making any special effort, absorb a great deal of radiant theoretical wisdom.

Intellectuals don't think; they have already thought. They have figured things out once and for all, and see the world through the delicate pink cotton candy of the theories they have spun. Airheads, on the other hand, never need to think at all. Theories and doctrines are laid out for them, like clothing for a young child by a thoughtful mother. They slip right into their nice neat clothes every morning and head forth to romp. See how happy the president looks in his!

Not all thinkers or educators are intellectuals. Artists obviously think, and some are regular full-bore thinkers. Paul Johnson absolves Edmund Wilson of being an intellectual on the grounds that he was actually a "man of letters."[19] Such a man knows, reads and thinks as much and as deeply as any intellectual, and might be just as much of a theory spinner. But he is too attached to the nuanced details that make some particular man or mood different from all others to be an intellectual. Mary McCarthy, at one time Wilson's wife, was fascinated by intellectuals because she lived among them, was easily seduced by their blandishments, and could pass for one herself. Yet McCarthy is also pronounced not guilty; she was "not a political animal at all," writes Johnson, "not really interested in ideas but in people."[20] (The author and (undoubted) intellectual Elizabeth Hardwick calls McCarthy a "woman of letters," and on that basis alone she is—according to Johnson—not guilty.)

There's also a type of educator whose approach is school-masterly rather than intellectual. The schoolmaster might be an artist or scientist or man of letters, but cares also about teaching and approaches it in a particular way—as if it were sacred. The schoolmaster cares about education not just in detail, in his own classroom, but in the large: how is society educating the next generation? He sees himself in historical context. He reveres tradition (not uncritically) and is in that sense conservative. In *Jude the Obscure*, one of Thomas Hardy's characters calls Oxford University "a nest of commonplace schoolmasters whose characteristic is timid obsequiousness to tradition."[21] Unfair. No schoolmaster at Oxford (or Harvard or Yale) is obsequious. He feels the majesty of the institution and is borne up by it, driven forward like a fine sailboat before the breeze. But Hardy's sense of the schoolmaster as admiring tradition and having no wish to be loud or bold-colored is true. The schoolmaster might be brilliant, might be a genius, but is nonetheless mannerly, modest, underplayed. And underpaid. But a proper professor in the Oxford or Cambridge tradition is, after all, a gentleman of means. Homer and Horace and botanizing were never meant to be paying professions.

Mark Pattison, head of Lincoln College at Oxford in the late nineteenth century, wrote that "the separation between Jowett and myself [Jowett was master of Balliol] consists in a difference upon the fundamental question of University politics—viz Science and Learning v. Schoolkeeping."[22] Schoolmasters are apt to make more of teaching or "schoolkeeping" than intellectuals do, but intellectuals are not necessarily indifferent to teaching. It's only that intellectuals make no distinction between teaching and convincing, or teaching and arguing.

To an intellectual, teaching means winning the other person to your viewpoint. In a sense this is a compliment to college students, who are treated as full-fledged intellectual opponents—until they concede, whereupon they become junior colleagues. But it also means that many intellectuals see nothing wrong in turning their classes into argument and propaganda for their own views—and they do it as second nature, in all innocence. When they are accused of politicizing the classroom, their reactions are sometimes "who, me?" and other times "but how else could I possibly do it?"

"The adversary culture" is a phrase Lionel Trilling invented to describe the belligerence of modern intellectuals and culture-mongers. Irving Kristol notes that this is an old phenomenon, that opposition is oxygen to the intelligentsia, and to some artists too; for "artists and writers and thinkers . . . are outraged by a society that merely tolerates them, no matter how generously."[23] The adversary culture, the intellectuals' world, withers and dies without opposition, and that is what we have today at the core of America's universities: dead forests, still formidable and spiky with their trunks, branches and thorns, but without a leaf, seed, chirp or howl of life anywhere.

The two big events that made up the cultural revolution stand in a rich and weedy patch of history, surrounded by other events that are not quite as tall, but almost. These were cluttered, difficult years for America, a meadow full of rustling wildflowers and junked cars up on blocks, leaking fluid from their rusting guts. During these years, often beautiful, often ugly, there were countless other influences on American culture. The struggle for civil rights goes back to just after the Civil War. The pacifism and appeasement that colored the opposition to the Vietnam War were ancient ideas that had been modernized by the British in the two decades following World War I.

The antiwar movement stood proudly for everything that was right and just and fun and free and easy, against America in Vietnam, in favor of a North Vietnamese victory, in favor of Black Power. *Against*, above all, every manifestation of the old established American leadership (the *Establishment* for short) that had led America to triumph in history's most cataclysmic war—a war on two fronts at opposite ends of the globe, against vicious, barbaric enemies. A war that made America admired and even (briefly!) loved around the world. A war fought by nearly the whole country, at least vicariously. A war that made America thoroughly and deservedly proud. And young people, members of the Movement, had missed *the whole damned thing*. To be left out of the greatest production in history and live your childhood in its shadow, its deep dark shadow . . .

The movement to end America's war in Vietnam was a large event that has long made the cultural revolution itself hard to see. The war's sharp claws gouged wounds in American flesh that healed slowly and left scars that might never disappear. And it played a big part in radicalizing the U.S. cultural establishment.

That the liberal establishment came to oppose the war bitterly makes it hard to remember that America in Vietnam was a liberal idea—especially the militarily disastrous first phase, before Abrams replaced Westmoreland in command and Nixon replaced Johnson as president. But more than that, America in Vietnam represented just the same kind of heedless intervention by intellectuals in real life that was vigorously pursued by left-liberal intellectuals at home.

One of those interventionist schemes was the forced busing imposed, usually by court order, between the late 1960s and the early 1980s. As far as people could tell, it did no good whatever—although it did induce many white parents to pull their children out of public schools or just leave town. In 1978, the RAND think tank actually conducted a study to determine *why* white parents were opposed to forced busing. And racism was not the reason! (Yet the theory said it was! What is *wrong* with these crazy RAND people?) Parents were opposed because . . . they wanted their children nearby. They wanted them in neighborhood schools. *What kind of reason is that?* Don't these hicks understand that *the whereabouts of some random white child* can't possibly matter when *social justice* is at stake?

It takes a think tank brimful of intellectuals to discover, by means of meticulous data collection and analysis, what any ten-year-old could have told them free of charge.

Hamlet is the apotheosis of the intellectual. He is brilliant, witty, knowledgeable, a fund of information. He can't wait to leave the royal court and get back to the university at Wittenberg. Pondering constantly, mainly about himself, he treats people like dirt—not deliberately, just carelessly. "Get thee to a nunnery," he suggests sweetly to his erstwhile girlfriend, before he (accidentally) kills her father without compunction, and mocks her brother's grief at her graveside after she has been driven to distraction and suicide. "The cat will mew, and dog will have his day."

"Scatter-site public housing" was yet another late-1960s inspiration, in which stable ethnic communities were bombed with multi-megaton low-income housing projects. Those projects tend to destroy the value of other houses in the neighborhood—that is a fact; the world happens to work that way—and many middle-class people put their life savings in their homes. The projects tend to increase street crime: another mere fact, of no significance to the new establishment. Hannah Arendt puts the case plainly (but you can hear her patience wearing thin) in a 1968 letter:

> The trouble with the New Left and the old liberals is the old one—complete unwillingness to face facts, abstract talk, often snobbish and nearly always blind to anybody else's interest. . . .
>
> The hypocrisy is indeed monumental. Integrated housing is of course quite possible and absolutely painless on a certain level of income and education, and it is a fait accompli in New York precisely in the expensive apartment buildings. No trouble whatsoever. The trouble begins with the lower income groups, and this trouble is very real. In other words, those who preach integration etc. are those who are

neither likely nor willing to pay the price. And then
look down their educated noses upon their poor
benighted fellow citizens, full of "prejudices."[24]

The Vietnam War and the left-liberal domestic policies of the
late 1960s and the '70s were equally inventions of the newly
bold, newly powerful American intelligentsia. In fact, they were
two facets of the same war: the war of left-liberal intervention-
ists against reality; the war of clean, elegant, elevated theory
against messy fact. "They will hardly have the natural scientist's
patience to wait until theories are verified or denied by facts,"
Hannah Arendt says of policy-making intellectuals in government. "Instead they will be tempted to fit their reality—which,
after all, was man-made to begin with and thus could have been
otherwise—into their theory."[25]

Today, intellectuals still attack social problems or alleged problems with the sledgehammers and welding torches of their people-
blind theories. For example, Title IX is a 1972 law, an amendment
to the 1964 Civil Rights Act, that has to do with equal treatment
of men and women. Under this law, according to the bureaucratic
powers that be, the number of women in college sports must
equal the number of men. *So what* if that causes men's teams to
be junked all over the country? What are a few dozen, hundred,
thousand disappointed young men (who even knows how many?
who cares?)—what are these mere *individual lives* compared with
the noble fight for social justice?

Suppose that men just happen to like sports better than women
do? But how *could* men like anything better than women, or vice
versa? Such a thing isn't possible, because left-liberal theory (or
Big Brother, or the god of the intellectuals) tells us that men
and women are interchangeable—just as our child-intellectual
could see that the yellow so-called "rose" was no rose at all; just
as fighting in Vietnam by maximizing the count of Viet Cong
dead (instead of liberating occupied territory) had to be the right

way to do it, because the theory said so, and so did Robert McNamara (Berkeley '37, Harvard '39), McGeorge Bundy (Yale '40) and
Walter Rostow (Yale BA and PhD '40): solid-gold liberal intellectuals every one of them.

—————

Another fact makes the cultural revolution hard to see: names
stayed the same while meanings changed. There were elite colleges before and after the revolution—mainly the same ones
before and after: the Ivy League universities, a few small, tony
liberal arts schools, the Stanfords and Dukes, the University of
Michigans and a few other outstanding state schools. In the very
top ranks, only the Seven Sisters (Vassar, Smith and the rest)—formerly women's colleges—lost influence as the world went coed.
Basically the list of fancy, prestigious names stayed the same,
while the institutions were hollowed out like scraped squash, and
new ingredients packed into the old shells.

The top colleges used to be society colleges; they were taken
over by intellectuals. And yet they *remained* "society colleges" while
society itself was redefined by the cultural revolution. In 2001,
Austin Bramwell, who contributed an introductory piece to the
fiftieth-anniversary edition of William Buckley's *God and Man at
Yale,* wrote that over the last half century Yale had "lost its unrivaled
social cachet"[26] without getting anything distinctive in return. If
that were true, Yale would *actually* be no better than Harvard! But
today, Bramwell's claim seems false. Prominent families are still
eager to send their children to Yale, and the children are still eager
to go—not, Lord knows, to learn anything (most of them), still less
to become thinkers or scholars or scientists. They go to Yale to
become prominent, powerful, successful, and naturally (why not?)
rich and famous. And Yale, radicalized and intellectualized as it
has become, does a fine job of meeting their needs. Thanks to
Yale's magic wand, they emerge gold-plated and fairy-dusted.

Yale remains one of a small handful of the most successful society colleges in the country. But the elite society that Yale students aspire to join has changed.

There was a cultural elite, an establishment, before and after the cultural revolution. Before, it was basically conservative, as the old-time WASP elite (white, Anglo-Saxon, Protestant) had always been; after, it was left-liberal, as the intelligentsia had always been. To put it differently, WASPs were replaced at the helm of American culture by PORGIs—post-religious, globalist intellectuals. The PORGIs are followed in turn by the PORGI Airheads, or intellectual*izers,* who have passed through the schools and colleges and come out seeing the world just as they are supposed to. For the new establishment, they are freshly minted money in the bank. One day this nation will belong to the Airheads, who will carry out PORGI theories as faithfully and thoughtfully as a bucket carries water.

The new establishment is "post-religious" in the sense that God and Judeo-Christian religion don't strike most modern intellectuals as important enough to dismiss. Mostly they don't even reach the point of being atheists. On the other hand, it has long been understood that left-liberalism is itself a religion. This is the positive side of left, the low-calorie spiritual sweetener that improves the fresh-squeezed lemon juice of rage, alienation and envy.

Among intellectuals, the left-liberal religious faithful are often not merely pious but zealous, even fanatic. To conservatives, they seem irrational and intellectually unserious, unable to hold their own in political argument, often unwilling even to try—all too apt, when pressed, to slouch off in a sulk or flare up like a burnt-out lightbulb with no more watts to spare on *you.* There is a frazzled flash, a silence, then "let's talk about something else." Many conservatives have had the experience.

But the left-libs make up for it with passion and intensity. Left-liberalism is a *new* religion, a live volcano no more than a few hundred years old and still feeling its way and creating its shape from week to week (although in some respects—earth worship, the sacralization of homosexuality—it resembles ancient paganisms). Conservatives on their part never suffer from this tendency to transform political ideas into religious dogma. If they are religious-minded (and many are), they are apt to be Jews or Christians.

The new establishment came to power with many ideas preformed, but it was open to new ones too—in light of its vastly expanded power and scope and its new duties running American culture. More than any other event, the civil rights movement supplied the new establishment with the attitudes and ideas it used to take charge of American culture. But ideas aside, this new PORGI establishment differed from the old WASP one in a fundamental way. The WASP establishment saw itself as the nation's high end, the top of a vertical spectrum. PORGIs see themselves as separated by a cultural Grand Canyon from the nation at large, with Harvard and the *New York Times* and the Boston Symphony and science and technology and iPhones and organic truffled latte on their side—and guns, churches and NASCAR on the other. Spectrum, hell!

The old WASP establishment saw the future as a long process of nudging uncivilized Americans upward gently, gently through the WASPness spectrum; it was a smug and patronizing view, yet essentially benign. The PORGI establishment sees a future of hoisting people aloft and swinging them—via the great crane of the PORGIfied schools and universities—from Reactionary Ridge on the far side of the canyon all the way to PORGI Paradise. Until every last reactionary is gone, a state of culture war exists between opposite sides, which can't even communicate except at the top of their lungs.

———

Intellectuals didn't conspire to make the cultural revolution happen. They could not have forced the Great Reform if they had tried, because the WASP elite colleges were private institutions in the age before massive federal grants let the government sink its teeth in permanently. The reform happened because the WASP elite stepped aside. It was a remarkable event—either a heroic, self-effacing embrace of justice for its own sake, or an act of exhaustion. Or (most likely) a combination of the two, exhaustion and nobility. In 1957, William DeVane, the patrician WASP we have already met, wrote that "the college should be a model of intellectual communal life, and from that position should show its society a fuller, richer, more gracious way of life." In '57, the top universities were still under WASP control, but their faculties and student bodies were changing dramatically. DeVane's words are noble, generous and WASP: a *more gracious* way of life.[27]

Intellectuals did not foresee the cultural revolution either, or the profound symbiosis between the Great Reform of the colleges and the rise of the Imperial University. They didn't see it coming—no one did; but they were the winners. They have come out on top. Once vaguely despised by most Americans, once treated as un-American weirdos to be housed in the dusty attic or mildewed basement of American life, they wound up as captains of the supertanker of U.S. culture, charting its course—and despising the nation at large as much as the nation had once despised them. Everyone knows that Harvard hates America, and it seems unfair: America never hated Harvard! But it is fair, after all, because America *did* despise the intellectuals, and those once-despised-by-the-nation intellectuals are now running Harvard—and are merely returning the favor, with interest.

chapter two

Snapshot 1941: War, the Elite and the Thinkers

PUT THEM ON THE TABLE IN FRONT OF YOU: A BLACK-AND-WHITE PHOTO from early 1941—tall and narrow and shiny, yellowing slightly, with deckled-looking edges; and a candy-colored photo from 1968—square and faded, from a Kodak Instamatic a generation later. Let's step into 1941, and then return to the '68 snapshot after we've followed the deep changes that separate these two eras.

In January 1941, the world is at war. America is not yet involved but the nation is tense, scanning every horizon; the sudden collapse of France shook America to the core. That mood lingers—like the smell of ash where some tremendous fire raged long ago—in the title of a piece by Janet Flanner in the *New Yorker*, December 1940: "Paris, Germany." The warlike, ominously smiling Japanese empire has occupied Manchuria and is now fighting a second war in China. In fall 1940, President Roosevelt asked for and got America's first peacetime draft. Starting in October, men between the ages of twenty-one and thirty-five are randomly chosen for twelve months of service. (Duty was extended when America entered the war, and men became eligible starting at eighteen.) At noon on October 19, 1940, Secretary of War Stimson reached into a glass bowl and, in a dazzle of flashbulbs, drew the name of Yuen Chong Chan (18 Pell Street, Manhattan) to be the nation's first peacetime draftee. Chan announced that he was pleased to be picked, was considered a crack rifle shot by his friends (shooting galleries were a favorite urban amusement), and couldn't wait to start battling Japan.[1]

Many thoughtful liberals were urging America to get into the European war, where Britain all alone faced a Nazi empire that had already crushed Czechoslovakia, Poland, Denmark, Norway, the Netherlands, Belgium and France. Right-wing isolationists demanded neutrality. The opposition of such famous right-wingers as Charles Lindbergh and groups like the America Firsters is well known. Right-wing opposition (sometimes stained with anti-Semitism) has a prominent place in modern history books.

Less well known are the left-liberal intellectuals who opposed American aid to Britain and, naturally, America's entering the fight herself. Mainly they were Marxists or socialists who saw the war, or pretended to see it, as a fight among capitalist, imperialist powers—a fight of no concern to America. (Not many Americans of any sort were sympathetic to the British Empire, as opposed to the British nation.) Some anti-Hitler sentiment within the U.S. intelligentsia magically evaporated when Stalin made his deal with Hitler one week before the Nazi invasion of Poland. Loyal American Communists followed Moscow's line. But there was principled antiwar sentiment too.

In fall 1939, a statement appeared in *Partisan Review*. *Partisan* (as people called it) ranks among the most important periodicals in modern history. It has "come to be regarded," wrote Diana Trilling in her memoirs (1993), "as the best intellectual journal of the American mid-twentieth century."[2] Norman Podhoretz called it "the most distinguished literary magazine of our time."[3] Irving Kristol wrote that "in its heyday" *Partisan* was "unquestionably one of the finest American cultural periodicals ever published—perhaps even the finest."[4] Cynthia Ozick remembered browsing a newsstand on her first day at college. "Copies of *Partisan Review*: the table of the gods. Jean Stafford, Mary McCarthy, Elizabeth Hardwick, Irving Howe . . . "[5] Many of the most eminent writers of the day. Here is *Partisan*'s view of the Second World War in fall 1939:

> The last war showed only too clearly that we can have no faith in imperialist crusades to bring freedom to any people. Our entry into the war, under the slogan of "Stop Hitler!", would actually result in the immediate introduction of totalitarianism over here. . . . The American masses can best help [the German people] by fighting at home to keep their own liberties.

Partisan called the statement "a letter to our readers," but it was signed by several contributors also, including some of the most prominent thinkers and writers of the era: the philosopher and education theorist John Dewey, the poet William Carlos Williams, the art critic Clement Greenberg, the art historian Meyer Schapiro, and others.

Also in fall '39, *Partisan Review* published a symposium in which distinguished writers were asked, among other things, to reflect on the approaching Second World War. Assuming the writers composed their answers that summer, Hitler had already remilitarized the Rhineland, occupied Austria, demanded and got (at the infamous Munich conference) the mountainous border region that protected Czechoslovakia from the Reich, and then rolled into Prague and occupied the rest of Czechoslovakia. On Kristallnacht in fall '38, synagogues had been burned, Jewish businesses looted and destroyed, and thousands of Jews carted off to the Dachau concentration camp. And Hitler was making no secret of his designs on Danzig and the Polish Corridor.

Diana Trilling summarized the symposium results: "Henry Miller [the novelist] sees 'no problem confronting the world which might not be solved peaceably'"—presumably, as world problems had been peacefully solved at Munich. "Sherwood Anderson submits that, as a literary man, he does not believe in any war: 'In a time of war any man working in the arts is sunk. His lamp is out.'" Anderson was the distinguished novelist. "Louise Bogan [the poet] writes: 'In the event of another war, I plan to oppose it with every means in my power.' James Farrell cheerily cites the Albanian who during the last war was asked how he felt about it and replied: 'What? Two dogs are fighting for a bone, and you ask the bone how it feels?'" Farrell was the author of the Studs Lonigan novels. "The response of Robert Penn Warren was the most economical and graphic: 'I think that if we get into the next war we are suckers.'" Warren was the novelist, poet, critic and eventual American poet laureate.

Even Lionel Trilling himself, who was known in later years for wisdom and prudence, "avoids any out-and-out statement against the impending war in Europe [his wife reports] and, like all the contributors, he fails to mention Hitler—nowhere in the symposium is there a hint of recognition of the true character of Naziism."[6]

And the intelligentsia acted on these convictions. "By one means or another," Mrs. Trilling wrote in 1993 about the era of the Second World War, "most of the intellectuals of our acquaintance evaded the draft."

The immediate introduction of totalitarianism over here: thus *Partisan Review* in its letter to readers imagined the consequence of America's entry into the war. The idea was absurd. But listen to Norman Mailer in 1968: "We are engaged in a war [Vietnam] which may go on for twenty years. Nothing less is involved than whether America becomes a great nation or a totalitarian tyranny."[7]

Intellectuals learn slowly. But one important thing *had* changed between *Partisan Review* in 1939 and Norman Mailer in 1968: the intelligentsia had taken over the establishment.

In 1940, the antiwar positions of left-wing intellectuals had virtually no resonance on college campuses, either among professors or among students facing the draft. Although the idea of America's entering the war was widely unpopular in the country and on campus, the colleges remained quiet. At Yale in those months between the start of the draft and Pearl Harbor, people evidently liked to say, "They don't draft Yale men, they just ration them."

A generation later, in 1968, things are fundamentally the same among intellectuals, but radically different at colleges like Yale. Once again, leading left-lib intellectuals oppose American involvement in war—with far more unanimity, if not more fervor, than they opposed American entry into World War II. But in 1968, the faculties of elite universities are a cheering section for American intellectuals, and a safe haven for many. In short: the second time around, intellectuals and top colleges will be of one mind on America and the war.

A huge and portentous change. How did it happen?

It happened like this: two big waves that were traveling in the same direction accidentally tumbled together and became one enormous wave. The two were the Great Reform of the colleges and the rise of the Imperial University. Together they made the cultural revolution that crashed on the beaches in the late 1960s and is still skimming upward—a great load of seawater that traveled so far and fast it covered the beach, surged round the dunes, flooded the parking lots, and then set off hunting through the towns and streets and homes of America, rearranging this nation forever.

The Great Reform turned the society college of 1940 into the intellectuals' college of 1970. The Harvards and Princetons, Vassars and Smiths, Benningtons and Amhersts of 1940 were mainly social and not intellectual lighthouses, luminous with high-watt exclusivity, beacons of classiness to the nation at large.

They were the final training grounds, the advanced flight schools for young American social leaders before these dauntless junior WASPs took to the air for their long flights over the valleys and up the mountains of American life. But the society college of 1940 revealed itself to be the mere chrysalis out of which the butterfly of the modern intellectuals' college would emerge, as gaudy as the WASP caterpillar had been discreet.

Meanwhile, another bracing breeze was transforming the staid old conservative colleges: the growing academic imperium was magnifying and expanding their influence over American life. Not only did the social lighthouses become intellectual lighthouses; their towers and lenses changed too. Now their beams picked out every corner of American culture; swept nearly the whole of American life. More and more Americans wanted and needed a bachelor's degree, and the influence of graduate and professional schools increased mightily too, as professionalization and specialization worked their changes on American life.

The result was a whole culture that moved leftward, a large fleet weighing anchor and sailing off; and then, instead of settling down, it continued drifting lefter and lefter, because that's where the new establishment, the cultural elite, was leading. Of course there are many flavors of left, some as different as sailboats and missile cruisers, but deep down they all share basic principles.

Many events besides the cultural revolution helped make America's mood, and many circumstances contributed to that revolution. But we can't understand America, or the past, or anything at all unless we are able to focus on certain facts—the most important—and temporarily ignore the rest. That's what I will do: focus on the cultural revolution and its two main causes, the Great Reform of the colleges and the rise of the Imperial University.

———

America's cultural revolution resonates on the soundboard of twentieth-century history with other important events at the same pitch. Britain gave up her empire—as France did too, but France was forced out while Britain might, in some cases, have stayed. Western Europe gradually dissolved her armies and stood down. Most important of all, in the decades following World War II, Europe turned out the lights and closed the door on Christianity—right after two mildly but consistently Christian nations, America and Britain, had fought off the most ferocious pagan regimes in history, Nazi Germany and imperial (officially state-Shinto) Japan, and were about to face down the third in Soviet Russia. *Was* Britain still a Christian nation in 1940? In *The Idea of a Christian Society* (1939), T. S. Eliot grudgingly conceded the point: Britain was "still Christian."[8] In 1941, George Orwell laid the facts on the table with his usual clarity: The "common people" of England "have retained a deep tinge of Christian feeling, while almost forgetting the name of Christ."[9]

The Second World War provided, at long last, the historical vindication that Judeo-Christian religion had sought unsuccessfully for two thousand years. Two Christian nations saved the world while two pagan nations plumbed the lowest depths of hell. But for Europe, it was too late.

(Of course the Soviets played a large part in the Allied victory—only to substitute Stalinist for Nazi hell.)

Western European culture today is just as intellectualized as American culture; far more so, in fact. It is run by PORGIs just as American culture is. And yet there was no Great Reform of the colleges in Europe, and no civil rights movement to ignite the brandy on the revolutionary crêpes suzette. How can the American cultural revolution be so important, when Europe arrived at the same location without bothering to have one?

America profoundly influences Western Europe. The massive Paris protest of students and intellectuals in May 1968 was wound up and set going, in significant part, by Americans protesting the Vietnam War. Elsewhere, "what the rebellious Italian students seem to be protesting against is mainly the war in Vietnam. . . . Freedom, in fact, is the last thing they consider or care about."[10] American student protests set off similar demonstrations all over Western Europe. To be against the Vietnam War in Western Europe was like being a fan of the trendiest rock band going—on top of which, you got to "clash with police" and know the thrill of virtue and danger. (Eastern Europe felt differently. In 1968, invading Soviet tanks had pinned down and flattened the living body of the latest Prague Spring. It was not pretty. Eastern Europe was not rooting for a Communist victory in Vietnam; it was pining, instead, for the victorious Communists to go away.)

And a more important underlying fact: European culture has always been intellectualized, with a long tradition of respect for intellectuals and professors that America lacks. European culture backed away from Christianity further and earlier than any major group of American Christians, and has had strong post-national or globalist urges since the end of the First World War. Europeans had undertaken colonialism, imperialism and Christian proselytizing on a greater scale than Americans did, and such activities brought about an earlier crisis of confidence among European intellectuals and Europeans generally.

One way to describe the results of America's cultural revolution is that America has become, in many respects, Europeanized. "It is the final consummation of an American," wrote T. S. Eliot, "to become, not an Englishman but a European—something no born Englishman, no person of European nationality can become."[11] Americans can be true Europeans because they can master European culture and yet transcend European nationalism. Of course, Eliot characteristically ignored the fact that European Jews had achieved this distinction long before he ever thought of it. Rarely accepted as bona fide nationals of any European state, Jews were nonetheless co-creators of European thought, along with the ancient Greeks, and they spoke with authority on European arts and letters, history and science. But Americans long ago pulled loose from Europe and invented a new nation, struggled to build it, and became the most productive (economically, intellectually) and freest nation in history. After all that, to allow America lamely to return, bleating, to the European flock—what a defeat for mankind!

But now we are ready. Bring on the revolution.

chapter three

The Great Reform

IN 1940, THE MISSION OF THE TOP COLLEGES WAS SOCIAL: TO ALLOW THE WASP elite to reproduce itself. Education in science and scholarship was part of the task, but subordinate to molding citizens who knew how to behave, how to distinguish themselves and set an example to the rest of society. Everyone assumed that future American leaders—of the government, the military, industry, the arts, society at large—would resemble past leaders in being overwhelmingly white, Anglo-Saxon males. But the same basic goals held at the tony girls' schools. In 1936, Wellesley started a new scholarship program aimed at "girls of fine character, mental keenness and qualities of leadership." Character first.

Aside from a very few important Catholic colleges, the elite schools were WASP institutions; most of the students and professors were WASPs. And not just any WASPs: they came from good families, usually with money. Prime candidates for admission were prospective social and not intellectual leaders—although brains were a useful bonus, and many freshmen emerged from their prep schools better educated than the college graduates of today. Leading professors and university officers were social figures. Some were sportsmen; many belonged to good clubs; they attended fashionable churches and gave their daughters society weddings. And all this was perfectly natural, because their families had built these places and supported them, served as their trustees and fundraisers and fund-givers as well as their provosts and presidents, bequeathed to them books and art and money and their own posh names to be chiseled into the stone of substantial, serious buildings. In the late 1930s, the *March of Time* newsreel referred to "America's colleges" as "quiet backwaters in a troubled world," and that's just how the old establishment liked them.

There were some Catholics (mainly from Northern European backgrounds), far fewer Jews and even fewer blacks at America's top-tier universities, and they were expected to fall in with the dominant WASP culture. Edmund Wilson met F. Scott Fitzgerald at Princeton in the 1910s; Fitzgerald, wrote Wilson, was "the first educated Catholic I had ever known."[1] The colleges of the old elite were conservative. Compulsory chapel was first abolished at the University of Wisconsin in 1869, but it survived until 1926 at Yale, "where graduating seniors regularly voted in favor of retaining it"[2] (partly, no doubt, out of spite). Princeton scaled back its twice-a-day Sunday chapel to once-a-day in 1882, but once-on-Sunday for underclassmen lasted officially until 1964. The Princeton of Edmund Wilson's day existed "between the pressures of narrow Presbyterianism and a rich man's suburbanism."[3]

We look at old-time WASP exclusivity as bigoted, and it was. But for the most part, after all, we do as we are taught, and as our elders and peers do.

F. Scott Fitzgerald is a good place to start understanding the society college; he entered Princeton in 1913 and wrote about it in novels and stories. What made a boy want to attend Princeton? Amory, the hero of *This Side of Paradise*, "had decided definitely on Princeton" during his last year at St. Regis, his prep school. "Yale had a romance and glamour from the tales of . . . St. Regis' men who had been 'tapped for Skull and Bones,' but Princeton drew him most, with its atmosphere of bright colors and its alluring reputation as the pleasantest country club in America."[4] Wellesley was another of those pleasant country clubs. "Wellesley girls" in the 1930s "donned their long black velvet evening coats, or their longer afternoon dresses that had replaced the knee-length models, and their Empress Eugénie hats, to go to dance to Leo Reisman's music at the Egyptian Room at the Brunswick . . . or to the new night clubs that were opening up."[5]

Yale and Princeton were the ranking society colleges, both of them more glamorous than Harvard and the rest of the Ivy League. Yale and Princeton ranked at the top partly because they were close to Manhattan, while Harvard was only close to Boston. Princeton was smaller and more exclusive, but Yale generally finished first. "In my youth it seemed so dynamic from Princeton," wrote Edmund Wilson.[6] Part of Yale's glitter came from the long-lost glamour of the Broadway stage: many New York plays tried out in New Haven. (New Haven and its famous Schubert Theater are part of *All About Eve* (1950) and *The Bandwagon* (1953), among other big Hollywood movies from the days when Broadway mattered.)

The three together—Harvard, Yale, Princeton—represented the sublime summit of American education. An unsophisticated Midwesterner in a Sinclair Lewis story "pictured Harvard and Yale and Princeton as ancient groves set with marble temples." They spoke to the American desire—a small but persistent itch—for ancient, noble institutions of the sort for which England was famous. The top three colleges had all been created before the Revolutionary War, had grown famous and venerable, and displayed on their noble breasts (like a trio of dowagers covered with family jewels) many quaintly idiosyncratic traditions, much cherished in a nation that always felt itself falling short in the quaintly idiosyncratic traditions department.

The three bigs were in a class by themselves in a 1951 survey showing "sharp differences in median income" among alumni of different schools. In a list of clusters ranked by median income per cluster, "the Big Three (Harvard, Yale, Princeton)" came first, then "other Ivy League," followed by "seventeen technical schools," then "twenty famous Eastern colleges," then "the Big Ten," and so forth.[7] (These clusters were invented beforehand, and the survey compared clusters rather than individual schools.) High median income reflected not only education and school environment but the sort of student who attended each college in the first place.

The Ivies were all men's schools until the 1960s. The Seven Sisters were women's liberal arts colleges that behaved like female Ivies. In fact, two were located right next to Ivies: Barnard at Columbia and Radcliffe at Harvard. The other five—Bryn Mawr, Smith, Mount Holyoke, Vassar and Wellesley—were also Northeastern, like the Ivies; and the atmosphere and social policies of the Ivies were mostly replicated at the Sisters. A 1957 study remarks matter-of-factly that "the high costs" at most women's colleges had "limited enrollment pretty largely to the upper income brackets."[8]

When a heroine (Vassar '33) of Mary McCarthy's novel *The Group* (1963) visualizes an absolutely standard "broker or a banker or a coldfish corporation lawyer," the type everyone expects her to marry (although she isn't going to), she sees him as "Yale or Princeton '29." But most of the eight Vassar '33 heroines of *The Group* are as class-conscious as their parents could wish. "He comes from a very good family," one of them reassures her mother about a boyfriend named Brown, "descended from Hawthorne. Brown is a very good name." Nonetheless, the Vassar heroines "could see the good Roosevelt was doing, despite what Mother and Dad said"[9]—a notably progressive position; after all, this was an era, Irving Kristol notes, "when most college students identified themselves as Republicans."[10] In Randall Jarrell's novel *Pictures from an Institution* (1954), "Many a Benton girl went back to her nice home, married her rich husband . . . ."[11] ("Benton" was loosely modeled on Sarah Lawrence.) McCarthy herself is winningly frank about these questions in her various volumes of memoirs. Speaking of one early lover, she reports that "Mangold, with his Yale background, was more my kind of person" than Philip Rahv, the brilliant Jewish intellectual who had never gone to college.[12]

Norman Podhoretz describes Columbia in 1914, long before he himself was an undergraduate there: "Columbia was the college of Old New York society—a kind of finishing school for young gentlemen who would soon enter the governing elite of the nation."[13] There were also tony liberal arts schools that ranked with the Ivies in the Northeast. In "Bernice Bobs Her Hair," Fitzgerald discusses "Warren McIntyre, who casually attended Yale," and Genevieve Ormonde, "who regularly made the round of dances, house-parties, and football games at Princeton, Yale, Williams, and Cornell."[14] Williams, Amherst, Swarthmore and a few other colleges and non-Ivy universities made the grade, as did MIT. And of course there were elite colleges outside the Northeast, from Duke and Johns Hopkins all the way out to Stanford.

The elite schools' reputation had other facets. Sinclair Lewis, tremendously popular as a novelist from the 1920s through the 1950s, had gone to Yale from Minnesota. He felt like an outsider and hated it—although he did become editor of the *Yale Lit*. Apparently, Yale didn't mind *him*. In a satirical Lewis story, an elderly Midwestern farmer becomes a student at Yale after reading a novel about the place "in which a worthy young man 'earned his way through' college, stroked the crew, won Phi Beta Kappa, and had the most entertaining, yet moral, conversations" with his friends. The farmer discovers that students who are "earning their way through" are just as vacuous as the wealthy kind, but finally finds one lone oddball who has enough sense for the hero to make friends with him.[15]

Yale offers a good picture of the prewar society college. It happens to be where I teach and was a student myself; and the social policy behind Yale admissions has been discussed in a number of studies. More important, Yale and Princeton were the iviest of the Ivy League. Before the Great Reform, no college was closer than Yale to the government and the old establishment. After the Second World War, no Ivy League school stuck longer to anti-Jewish bigotry. But when the cultural revolution hit, Yale swung hard left.

In 1939, "the Yale man" was an admired type—not on account of intellect or learning, but for gentlemanly savoir-faire. Tom Wolfe reminisces in *Radical Chic* (1968): "He looks like the intense Yale Man from out of one of those 1927 Frigidaire ads in *The Saturday Evening Post,* when the way to sell anything was to show Harry Yale in the background, in a tuxedo, with his pageboy-bobbed young lovely, heading off to dinner at the New Haven Lawn Club."[16]

Yale's president in 1939 was Charles Seymour, who was simultaneously a scholar with a Yale PhD and a Superwasp (a social type, not a comic-book hero). As with many other Superwasp presidents, his old-school roots went deep: Seymour was descended from two Yale presidents (of the 1740s and the 1820s), and from many generations of Yale students going back to the founding of the college in 1701. As a Yale student himself he'd made Skull and Bones, and afterward became an expert advisor to American diplomats during the writing of the Paris Peace Treaty following the First World War.

Skull and Bones, along with the other Yale "secret societies," recruited campus leaders. There were no Jews and *a fortiori* no blacks in Bones until the late 1940s, when the reform was already under way. No other Ivy League school had Yale-style secret societies (Skull and Bones, Scroll and Key, and Wolf's Head are the oldest), each with its own elaborate clubhouse on campus. These buildings are instantly recognizable because they are windowless but evidently not mausoleums, which are rarely found in the middle of urban blocks. They sprang up like rare, stately mushrooms after a long and drenching rain (of money). Each society has its own endowment and top-secret laws, rituals, ceremonies, codes, handshakes, passwords, large stables, fabulous possessions, vast hunting preserves, luxurious offshore palaces, small private countries on the Riviera near Monaco, treasure chests of jewels for each new member, and *enormous* harems, constantly replenished! Of course, this account is partly speculative, because the secret societies are, after all, *secret*. But any undergraduate can tell you that being a member of Bones is just like being king of France in 1677, only much better.

These societies were—still are—a perfect symbol of the elite universities' relationship to America at large, both before and after the reform: they hold the commonality at arm's length. The public is invited to keep out. *Odi profanum vulgus, et arceo.* "I loathe the vulgar masses, and keep them at a distance." (Horace, *Odes* III:1.) Yet these strange institutions with their vivid buildings are part of Yale's lovable crankiness. The university invented itself step by step, with imagination and flair, and its character (discreetly histrionic) has always been distinctive. For "those who had proudly belonged to the best senior societies and fraternities," Edmund Wilson wrote, "Yale was a kind of religion."[17]

In "Portrait of the Intellectual as a Yale Man," Mary McCarthy writes of her hero that "he could have been Bones but wouldn't." Only an ultra-radical on the ragged edge of sanity would turn down such an offer. Although the hero was an aspiring Marxist intellectual, "his rough-and-tumble vocabulary was a sort of apology to the gods of decorum, who must have appeared to him in the guise of football players."[18] Naturally, football was an important part of Yale life. Cole Porter, enrolled in the class of 1913, was a member of Scroll and Key; he sang in the Whiffenpoofs, "gentleman songsters off on a spree," and wrote fight songs for the football team. Scott Fitzgerald traces the tradition back to the previous century, in a story about "the sort of college student who in the early nineties drove tandems and coaches and tallyhos between Princeton and Yale and New York City to show that they appreciated the social importance of football games."[19] In the 1890s, we learn elsewhere, forty-five Yale graduates, thirty-five Princetonians and twenty-four Harvard alums were teaching the newfangled game of football throughout the country.[20] Football had been invented at Yale, with odd snippets of advice (surprisingly unhelpful) from the other Ivies.

Princeton had no secret societies but did have eating clubs, which were almost as good. Like all top-quality clubs, these had clout. In his junior year, Fitzgerald's hero Amory knows he's arrived when members of Ivy, Tiger Inn and the Cottage come calling to check him out. "Unknown men were elevated into importance when they received certain coveted bids; others who were considered 'all set' found that they had made unexpected enemies, felt themselves stranded and deserted, talked wildly of leaving college."[21]

The close connection between the Yale man and America's leadership went without saying. Today's Yale graduates are also presumptive leaders of the American establishment—but the new establishment is different from the old. One sign of the difference is that pre–cultural revolution Yale men who were interested in government jobs were drawn to the military and to U.S. spy agencies, not only to political and diplomatic positions. Old Yale's many connections with the CIA and its forerunners involved not just alumni recruits but professors lending their foreign-affairs expertise. The university's proclivity for spying goes back to Nathan Hale (Yale 1773); the statue of Hale outside CIA headquarters in Langley, Virginia, is a copy of Yale's own.

In the 1950s, the CIA was said to be especially rich in Bonesmen. Norman Mailer's beautifully written and carefully researched half-novel *Harlot's Ghost* (1991) is about the CIA in the 1950s and early '60s. The young hero is a Yale man in the CIA; his father was also a Yale man in the CIA and formerly in the OSS. Another recruit, a Jew who enlists at the same time, struggles to fit in. "Harlot," code name of the central character in the story, is modeled on the famous CIA man James Jesus Angleton, Yale '41. The real Angleton—fine-boned, penetrating gaze, searching eyebrows, owlish glasses, barest hint of a smile—looked uncannily like the creator of modern counterintelligence, which he was. During the Second World War, Angleton worked at the Office of Special Services, the CIA's forerunner. Angleton's OSS boss Norman Holmes Pearson was another Yale alum. Angleton ran counterintelligence until Seymour Hersh laid him low in 1974 with a series of *New York Times* exposés about the CIA's involvement in domestic spying.

Hersh, the crusading writer who combined reporting with propaganda and helped bend the steel beam of American journalism to the left, was a hero of the cultural revolution. His conflict with Angleton was (among other things) a conflict with old Yale: the new establishment vanquished the old, and dragged its corpse symbolically round and round Yale's Old Campus walls in triumph. Hersh, the son of Yiddish-speaking immigrants from Lithuania, defeated Angleton, the son of an American cavalry officer, Superwasp, Yale man extraordinaire.

In his definitive *Cloak and Gown: Scholars in the Secret War, 1939–1961* (1987), Professor Robin Winks of Yale concludes that the professionalization of the CIA in modern times discouraged the recruitment of youth who were schooled in patriotism and civic virtue at America's nobler universities. The old cozy connections between Yale and American intelligence are long gone.

There were always serious students at Yale, and serious courses. In some ways, Yale was more serious about education before the reform than it is today: the schoolmasterly tradition was strong at all the top colleges. Classes were often tougher than they are today. The surprise "ten-minute quiz," for example, was an institution at Yale and many other colleges into the 1960s; it is said to have evolved from prep-school practices. In the old days, nearly all Yale men came from prep schools. Many still do.

Fitzgerald describes one successful applicant to Princeton who "received the grade A—excellent" on his entrance exams, "in

Caesar, Cicero, Vergil, Xenophon, Homer, Algebra, Plane Geometry, Solid Geometry, and Chemistry." After finishing at Princeton, "he went up to Yale to take his degree as Master of Arts."[22] The Big Three did lots of business.

There were always intellectuals among the professors at leading colleges too. In effect, there were intellectuals' sanctuaries—nature preserves within the capacious walls of the society college where a select group of specimens was allowed to do as it liked.

Thus the famous example of Lionel Trilling at Columbia. He was a Jew teaching English, which was like a Zulu teaching Greek: no doubt there *are* notable Zulu classicists, but why hire one when you can hire a European Christian, an actual descendant of Greeks with the blood of Sophocles pounding in his veins? On top of that, Trilling was a Freudian and a Marxist. The English department refused him tenure in the mid-1930s and sent him on his way. Whereupon, in summer 1939, the very *president of the university,* Nicholas Murray Butler himself—Superwasp First Class, a national figure, apotheosis of the old-school university president—reached his powerful, distinguished hand down, down into the English department and, exercising his executive powers, *personally* awarded Trilling the Jew tenure as professor of English literature at Columbia University. The world gasped, not only at the audacity but, all things considered, the wisdom of this gesture. Nor am I ridiculing it. This was WASP stewardship at its most majestic.

Columbia was the scene of another, more typical case of impressive WASP stewardship of the intellectuals (and notably the Jews) among them. In 1914, Frederick Keppel, dean of the college, defended his Jewish undergraduates in the face of assertions that Columbia's "position at the gateway of European immigration makes it socially uninviting to students who come from homes of refinement." People would often ask, "Isn't Columbia overrun with European Jews who are most unpleasant persons socially?" Keppel replied, "The Jews who have had the advantages of decent social surroundings for a generation or two are entirely satisfactory companions." As for the rest, "some of these are not particularly pleasant companions, but the total number is not large," he said, and added that Columbia "must stand ready to give to those of probity and good moral character the benefits which they are making great sacrifices to obtain."[23] Nowadays we are quick to denounce such a statement as bigoted, but look again: it is also true. And that poses a problem for the modern establishment: can a statement be simultaneously bigoted *and* true?

Things would have been different if the old schoolmasterly elite had stayed on to run these institutions and oppose the intellectual profs in the name of tradition and courtesy, strict standards and intellectual freedom and love of country. But such a world would have been no more stable than a ball balanced on the tip of a pyramid. Once the intellectuals started to run admissions and faculty hiring, the alumni—having passed through the faculty filter and been purified—were bound to think, for the most part, like their teachers; and the old ways couldn't possibly have remained.

The big change that made over the elite colleges was no swallows-to-Capistrano-style migration of intellectuals from American cities to the campuses. Some intellectuals did leave (or add to) their jobs as editors, staff or freelance writers, journalists and so forth by joining faculties. Philip Rahv, for instance, one of the creators and editors of *Partisan Review,* joined the faculty at Brandeis in the 1950s; his coeditor, William Phillips, went to Rutgers in 1963. Freelance writers and intellectuals also became increasingly frequent visitors at universities in the 1950s and '60s, delivering lectures or guest courses.

But the most important change was in interests and susceptibilities: a new generation of students and professors, including many previously unwelcome types, were attuned to the work of intellectuals; they admired and wanted to emulate intellectuals. As the old social and schoolmasterly missions lapsed, elite colleges took up a new mission: to become centers and sounding boards for the theories of intellectuals; to become intellectualized; to renounce WASPdom for PORGIness.

Today there are a few conservatives at each elite American college, and they live in protected habitats like the ones the intellectuals used to inhabit. As Shakespeare's most acerbic clown remarks toward the end of *Twelfth Night*, "And thus the whirligig of time brings in his revenges."

———

I will use American Jews as carbon 14: a way to trace the enormous change in America's elite colleges, and the course and consequences of the cultural revolution. Jews didn't cause these big changes; they are too scarce on the ground. But we can use the Jews to trace large changes. Here are some facts.

At the beginning of the cultural revolution, Jews were a small presence in the student bodies and faculties of the elite universities, and nonexistent among deans and provosts and presidents. A novel from 1952 records a casual comment at a faculty meeting: "A Jewish college, like Brandeis, will naturally hire Jewish applicants, since most other colleges discriminate against them."[24] *Naturally.* Bigotry at WASP colleges reflected WASP bigotry in general—not the sort that was guilty of pogroms or lynching, but the smooth and easy variety, Bigotry Lite, for fastidious anti-Semites; it merely posts signs reading "Keep Out." W. H. Auden wrote in 1946 that "The American Country Club . . . is both inexcusable and vulgar, for, since it purports to be democratic, its exclusion of Jews is a contradiction for which it has to invent dishonest rationalizations."[25] Of course, country club and college were two types of one institution: in both, the all-important admissions committee had to construct a social world it approved and enjoyed, for itself and for its children.

By 1970, the world had changed. Jews were a major presence among students and professors at the elite universities, and starting to make their presence felt in administration too. As the

Jewish presence at top colleges shot up and burst into bloom, three Jewish attributes stayed the same:

1. Politically, American Jews are far to the left of the main-stream. (Thus Milton Himmelfarb's famous observation that Jews earn like Episcopalians and vote like Puerto Ricans.)
2. Culturally, Jews have always admired intellectuals.
3. The Jewish way of argument is expert and aggressive.

Naturally, we would expect that an increasing Jewish presence at the top colleges would have these consequences:

1. The colleges would move left politically.
2. They would move closer to the intellectuals' worldview—become increasingly intellectualized.
3. They would acquire a more thrusting, belligerent tone.

And this is just what happened. If the one thing we knew about postwar American society were the changing relationship of Jews to elite universities, we would have to expect a change in American culture: a leftward breeze. A slightly more intellectualized tone. And at the colleges, a less restrained presentation of views.

Of course, what happened was more than a breeze. It was a hard gale, toppling boats into huge seas, generating waves that chased each other and crashed tumbling together—waves of change created by the top universities, propagated through mainstream culture, and eventually washing ashore as big breakers on the quiet beaches of everyday American life, continuing right into Barack Obama's presidency.

The distinctively Jewish worldview was important to this process. And *no,* obviously, not every Jew operates the same way, just as not every Gentile does. But Jews are the senior nation of the Western world; they have a continuous cultural history of perhaps three thousand years. Throughout this time, they were obsessed with literary and religious beauty and social justice and ethics and sanctity and God—which gave them plenty to talk about. It's only natural that they should have developed their own distinctive way of arguing.

The classic Jewish argument drills and blasts as deep as necessary, or deeper (the essence of Jewish genius is not knowing where to stop); it summons ideas from the ends of the earth to make a point. Such arguments, intense and belligerent and sometimes exhausting, would be intolerable if they weren't also funny. Humor is always latent in a classic Jewish argument, ready to strike in dry flashes, waiting quietly like static electricity curled up in a comfortable sweater.

"In the world of the 'Jewish establishment,'" writes Norman Podhoretz, "it was almost considered bad form, or a mark of low intelligence, to say anything kind in conversation about any other member of the group."[26] As Mary McCarthy penetrated the world of New York writers, she arrived at a party where "the guests were all intellectuals, of a kind unfamiliar to me. I could hardly understand them as they shouted at each other."[27] And again: "Rough plebeian democracy is the breeding-ground of the class of intellectuals, springing up like the dragon's teeth to fight and kill each other down to the last five men before they can found the city."[28] The people she means were mainly Jews.

The arguments of Jewish intellectuals assume an opponent, a counterforce. Podhoretz makes a revealing comment in *Breaking Ranks* about his uneasiness in the late 1950s with the "single-minded anti-Communism" of certain intellectuals at the time. "In the past there had been many defenders of the Soviet Union to argue against, but against whom was the argument being conducted in the present?"[29] Against no one; in the late '50s there *were* no credible defenders of the Soviet dictatorship. And yet the intellectuals to whom Podhoretz refers went on flailing mightily against an opponent who wasn't there.

The same thing happened on a much larger scale in the cultural revolution. As the 1960s wore on and the arguments of the newly powerful left-wing intelligentsia grew hotter and stronger and louder, no one predicted that the old establishment would strike its tents and fade away. But it did. Meanwhile, the new establishment kept on slamming punches. And instead of a match, there was a rout.

Of course, Jews have been as prominent in modern conservatism as in liberalism. The importance of such thinkers as Irving Kristol and Norman Podhoretz to contemporary conservatism is self-evident. (Elsewhere I have described Disraeli as the first modern conservative—the first to see conservatism as a governing philosophy for the whole nation and not merely for certain groups and special interests.) "Clarity is courage," Podhoretz writes; so let us be clear. Jewish intellectuals, *not as Jews but as intellectuals,* were an important part of the flood that washed away American culture as it used to be; and they ranked among the cultural revolution's most sophisticated, intelligent, articulate and belligerent voices.

Philip Roth, who has tracked his own passionate ambivalence about Judaism across dozens of novels and stories without ever running it down, writes in his memoir *The Facts* (1988) that Jews are sometimes described as neurotic when they are actually naïve. Jews tend to be "very naïve," he writes, "even the brightest, and not just as youngsters either."[30] Roth is a man of the left, and would surely insist that Jewish conservatives and not just Jewish liberals might easily be "very naïve." But since the large majority of Jews are liberal, we can only conclude that intense Rothian naïveté is more likely to produce liberals than conservatives.

—·—

The top colleges were wrong to keep Jews out just because they were Jews, as the colleges were wrong in all their bigoted ways.

The quota system that limited Jewish admissions at American universities was partly a response to short-term flare-ups in Jewish enrollments in the first decades of the twentieth century. By the early 1920s, the proportion of Jewish undergraduates at Harvard had reached just over 20 percent, compared with around 7 percent at the turn of the century. Jewish enrollments at Columbia briefly reached nearly 40 percent in the same period. Many other elite colleges also saw substantially increased Jewish enrollments. There were Jews everywhere! Gentiles were even required to be in the same room with them sometimes. Clearly, emergency procedures were required.

And so, in the early 1920s, officials at top colleges reacted by reducing Jewish enrollments and thereby preventing the cultural transformation of their colleges. Was this bigotry, was it prejudice? Of course. Robert Corwin, who designed Yale's anti-Jewish admissions policy, accused Jewish students of lacking "manliness, uprightness, cleanliness, native refinement, etc."[31] Note the *et cetera:* any competent anti-Semite was presumed capable of augmenting the list *ad infinitum*. But at the same time, anti-Jewish admissions policies were an attempt to maintain a thing these institutions valued highly and had every right to value: the mood or atmosphere or ambience of their campuses. (And remember that there were plenty of non-anti-Semitic WASPs.)

In 1922, Harvard's president A. Lawrence Lowell proposed a 15 percent quota on Jewish student admissions at the university as a whole. This quota, he said, would prevent anti-Semitism by keeping Jews from turning into a nuisance—just as the rising proportion of Jews at Harvard had been accompanied, he noted, by evidence of rising anti-Semitism. Harvard rejected the proposed explicit quota, but achieved the same thing by craftier means. A geographic distribution requirement in admissions cut Jews back to around 15 percent by the early 1930s—American Jews being concentrated in a few large cities at the time. Harvard's policy was affirmative action for rurals.

Yale's main technique for limiting Jews was an explicit preference, starting in 1925, for sons of alumni. The goal was a cutback
to 10 percent Jewish students, which was quickly accomplished.

Beginning with Harvard in 1926, the Ivies had another weapon in
their WASPness-protection arsenals: the Scholastic Aptitude Test.
The SAT required a more refined knowledge of English than old-
style admissions tests. Jewish candidates in these years were often
children of immigrants who had grown up in Yiddish-speaking
households; sometimes they were immigrants themselves. They
mastered English as a matter of course, but in some cases (only
some) not as fully as their children and grandchildren would.

And so, by various methods, the brief Jewish onslaught was
rolled back, without substantial losses. Elite WASPs everywhere
breathed a sigh of relief, and got back to fiddling with their spin-
nakers and canoes and other WASP things—snowshoes, moose
heads, liquor cabinets, etc. From the late 1920s through the late
1940s, the percentage of Jewish students in the Ivy League as a
whole is estimated at around 10 percent. (Jews were about 2 percent of the American population in 1900, over 3 percent in 1945,
and back down to less than 2 percent today.)

In the memorable opening of *The Sun Also Rises* (1926),
Hemingway describes an Ivy League Jew of the post–World War
I era:

> Robert Cohn was once middleweight boxing cham-
> pion of Princeton. Do not think that I am very much
> impressed by that as a boxing title, but it meant a lot
> to Cohn. He cared nothing for boxing, in fact he dis-
> liked it, but he learned it painfully and thoroughly to
> counteract the feeling of inferiority and shyness he
> had felt on being treated as a Jew at Princeton. There
> was a certain inner comfort in knowing he could
> knock down anybody who was snooty to him.

Jews who wanted to attend college before the reform were not stopped by bigotry. They just went to different colleges. Then as now, the Ivies and other top schools were pathways into the establishment—into powerful, wealthy, prestigious careers and the network of people who ran American culture, insofar as it *can* be run. But there were other ways to get educated.

In the 1920s through the '50s, and well into the '60s, Jewish students inundated the City University of New York. CUNY as such was organized only in 1961, but New York's many municipal colleges, graduate and professional schools came under a single governing board in the mid-1920s. CUNY's most important campus was the City College of New York, founded in Manhattan in 1847. City College (like the Ivies) was all-male. Manhattan's Hunter College for women was born in 1870, and set up outposts elsewhere in the city. Brooklyn College was organized in 1930, Queens College in '37; both were coeducational. CUNY's undergraduate schools charged city residents no tuition until 1975.

CUNY welcomed students the Ivies and Sisters didn't want. (Most couldn't have paid Ivy tuition anyway, without scholarships.) It also welcomed professors the Ivies had no use for. It's no surprise that Jews were a large presence among students and teachers there. And the results were intellectual distinction— among students more than teachers—and a pronounced leftward list.

CUNY was famous in the 1930s and '40s for its dim-lit basement lunchroom equipped with alcoves where arguments among undergraduates continued day to day, month to month, like the murmur of perpetual masses in medieval chantries: service at the altar of Political Argument never lapsed. Irving Howe, a CUNY alum and distinguished historian, writes that "anyone could join in an argument, there was no external snobbism, but whoever joined did so at his own risk, fools and ignoramuses not being suffered gladly."[32] Irving Kristol, a CUNY alum, a founder of the informal movement called neoconservatism and one of the most influential intellectuals of twentieth-century America, remembers "the physical squalor and mental energy of Alcove No. 1," which belonged to the Trotskyists. Garden-variety Communists had the next alcove down. "One argued incessantly, and generally devoted oneself to solving the ultimate problems of the human race," Kristol writes. "It was my involvement with radical politics," he explains, "that led me to read and think and argue with furious energy."[33]

When Yale decided to admit crowds of students who resembled CUNY intellectuals more than classical Yale men, the character of Yale changed, and eventually the character of America did too.

It's not clear that the exodus of smart students from New York's public colleges into fancy private schools did anyone much good in the end. Intellectually distinguished public colleges where tuition is low or free are an obvious public good. If more superior students had stayed at CUNY, it might have become one of the world's great universities.

———

If Jewish intellectuals were important to the cultural revolution, so were deluxe, top-drawer WASPs. After World War II, the old WASP academic leadership had no heart—or not much—to oppose the Great Reform, the step-by-step end of bigotry that was poised to transform the colleges. But the WASP role wasn't simply passive. Sometimes WASP leaders took the first steps of the Long March all by themselves. After the war, the halo around interventionist liberalism left by FDR's presidency and untimely death prompted important WASP academic leaders to start the revolution without waiting for the revolutionaries, by pushing their institutions leftward. Academia was in a liberal mood, and liberal-tending old-line WASPs were prominent among the mood makers. In fact, America at large was in a liberal mood. Lionel Trilling famously wrote, in the preface to *The Liberal Imagination* (1950), that "in the United States at this time liberalism is not only the dominant but even the sole intellectual tradition. For it is the plain fact that nowadays there are no conservative or reactionary ideas in circulation."[34]

William Buckley's celebrated *God and Man at Yale* (1951) describes a university that was already moving leftward when Buckley graduated in 1950. Charles Seymour had been Yale's president since 1937, when he had said in his inaugural address, "I call on all faculty freely to recognize the tremendous validity and power of the teachings of Christ in our life-and-death struggle against the forces of selfish materialism." But 1950 was a different world. Although *Time* magazine still regarded Yale as "a citadel of conservatism," Buckley as an undergraduate discovered differently: he found that Yale's "values" were on the whole "agnostic as to religion, 'interventionist' and Keynesian as to economics, and collectivist as applied to the relation of the individual to society and government." (This is how John Chamberlain, a prominent and powerful journalist, summarized it in the foreword he contributed to the first edition of *God and Man at Yale*.)

In modern terms, this is tame stuff. But official Yale didn't like these charges, and took to distributing the harshly negative review of Buckley's book that McGeorge Bundy had published in the *Atlantic*. Bundy called Buckley a "violent, twisted, and ignorant young man"[35]—which he wasn't; not even close. The strangely superfluous anger in this ugly accusation suggests the insider's rage at the ungrateful outsider. Who is this kid, anyway, with the nerve to defend *McGeorge Bundy's university* against McGeorge Bundy? Buckley, a Roman Catholic, had spoken up not for a Catholicized university but for old-fashioned WASP Yale.

Bundy was an old-line WASP and a driver of the cultural revolution from the very start, following World War II. He came from an old WASP family, graduated from Yale in 1940 (having made Skull and Bones, like his father), worked with distinction in intelligence during the war, and in 1953 became the youngest dean of faculty in Harvard's history. Then John Kennedy brought him to Washington. More than any other government intellectual, Bundy is associated with Lyndon Johnson's policy of steadily increased

U.S. military commitment to Vietnam: Bundy was *the* perfect Cold Warrior hawk. But in 1966 he left to become president of the Ford Foundation, and evidently had a change of heart. He drove the foundation steadily leftward, turning it into a dangerous, disruptive force in New York City racial and ethnic politics—so much so that Henry Ford II quit his own family's foundation in 1976. Bundy continued as foundation president until 1979.

McGeorge Bundy changed his opinions occasionally (don't we all?), but never changed his mind. He was a liberal interventionist from start to finish, the perfect paradigm of a left-lib intellectual in action. Had he been a Jew, he would have been called a self-hating one; instead he was a self-hating WASP, a distinguished representative of a major cultural revolutionary force, helping to unravel WASP dominance of the leading universities and the establishment generally.

Self-hating Jews are a famous breed, and have been a curse to the Jewish community throughout history. Self-hating WASPs are different: the worst that most of them ever faced was dislike; and their self-hatred was, accordingly, more a loss of self-assurance, mixed with a certain self-disdain. But it was real and important. Self-hating Jews love to rail against Zionism or Jews or Judaism, or all three. Self-hating WASPs are more discreet, softer-spoken, less emotional in their self-hatred; that's how WASPs are. (You've noticed?) But we must not be confused by this difference in external symptoms. We knew before we started that a self-hating WASP, if such a thing existed, could not possibly *seem* the same as a self-hating Jew.

Self-hating WASPs merely, quietly undermined WASP power and influence, and the power and influence of the United States. At a crucial moment in American history, they worked to topple the old WASP establishment and set PORGIs on the throne instead. Perhaps they did it out of a disinterested love of tolerance, perhaps out of fervent left-liberal beliefs, or perhaps out of self-hatred and no more. Or for all of these reasons, or none. *What it cost / Them is their secret.* This fragment of Robert

Lowell's harrowing "Quaker Graveyard in Nantucket" (1946) comes irresistibly to mind. Lowell was himself the type of the self-hating WASP, and a hero of the antiwar movement in the 1960s. He had bitterly opposed America's part in World War II also, and had been too honest to beat around the bush: he served five months in prison for refusing to enter the military in 1943. Again: there were strong antiwar voices among American intellectuals during World War II as well as Vietnam. But during Vietnam, college students were listening, and the establishment was transformed.

The *quintessential* self-hating WASP was a special case. He was a man of action, not just contemplation; he drove the cultural revolution from outside academia. Left-lib intellectuals hated this man even more than they did McGeorge Bundy, but once again they were unjust: he was one of them. Like Bundy he was a brilliant WASP intellectual who seemed to veer all over the map, from hard-right Vietnam hawk to globalist left-liberal. But he was the same man throughout, another WASP intellectual who helped make the cultural revolution and destroy the WASP establishment forever.

Robert McNamara was a star student at Berkeley in the mid-1930s and went on to Harvard for an MBA. He was an assistant professor at Harvard when the Second World War began. After many tries, he finally got the army to accept him despite his poor eyesight. He left the service as a lieutenant colonel in 1946 and never went back to teaching, but continued his work as a master of quantitative analysis. He went to the Ford Motor Company and rose to the top; but the McNamaras kept living in the college town of Ann Arbor, among University of Michigan folk, instead of the upscale Detroit suburb where wealthy Fordniks gathered. McNamara had been president of Ford for one month when JFK hired him away to be secretary of defense.

McNamara approached the growing war in Vietnam like the interventionist intellectual he was. Inevitably he made a tragic mess of it. In 1968 he left government to become president of the World Bank, which he ran on sturdily liberal principles until 1981.

In *The Best and the Brightest* (1969), David Halberstam called the World Bank job "the very antithesis of [McNamara's] previous position as head of the greatest war machine in the history of the world."[36] But in this new job, McNamara simply kept doing what he liked best: puppet-mastering, on the largest possible stage. He dreamed up the plans, did the analyses, and then pulled the strings from the executive loft far overhead. In 1995 he published a memoir in which he condemned his own conduct as defense secretary, and apologized for being "wrong, terribly wrong" about the war in Vietnam. The left refused to forgive him. But in the very starkness and intensity of his confession we hear the pain of a man turning against himself, hating himself. In a late poem, Robert Lowell's contrition blocked his throat. He was struggling. But he made it, unforgettably, to the end.

> I have sat and listened to too many
> words of the collaborating muse,
> and plotted perhaps too freely with my life,
> not avoiding injury to others,
> not avoiding injury to myself—
> to ask compassion . . . this book, half fiction,
> an eelnet made by man for the eel fighting
>
> my eyes have seen what my hand did.

Another heir presumptive of the old establishment who migrated into the new PORGI establishment was William Sloane Coffin. His uncle was president of Union Theological Seminary in Manhattan; his father was a wealthy businessman, and president of New York's Metropolitan Museum of Art. As university chaplain at Yale in the 1960s, William Sloane Coffin became a leader of the antiwar movement.

The president of Yale from 1963 to 1977 was Kingman Brewster, a lineal descendant of William Brewster, *Mayflower* Pilgrim and leader of Plymouth Colony. Kingman Brewster was another self-hating WASP: he was born and reared to be an old-style social leader, but became a convert to the new establishment and an implacable opponent of the old WASP elite. He was charming to everyone. I remember him sweeping into Commons (a huge, cold, hollow-feeling room) toward midnight at the Yale Prom, in his perfect evening clothes and formal cape. The instant he arrived, everyone knew somehow that he was there. When Brewster left Yale, President Jimmy Carter made him ambassador to Great Britain. It was the perfect job for him—and Carter was the perfect president to be his pal.

Yale made a symbolic transition when Bartlett Giamatti became president after Brewster in 1978. An eminent teacher and scholar, Giamatti was a professor of comparative literature at the university when he was chosen to be president. He made a fine president—and a fine commissioner of major league baseball after he left Yale; his interests were wide. But equally important were the things he was not: not a pillar of the WASP establishment, not even a WASP but a WIP, the Protestant grandson of Italian immigrants.

———

After the Second World War, most top colleges reacted very differently to the large numbers of Jewish applicants than they had in the previous generation. Elite colleges allowed an increasing influx of Jews, though sometimes grudgingly, knowing that cultural change would follow. But the colleges changed the students too. When Norman Podhoretz was an undergraduate at Columbia in the late 1940s and early '50s, there was still a quota for Jewish undergraduates (around 17 percent), but he didn't care. "Daniel Bell speaks of the 'conversion experience' which the college seems to induce in many of its students," he writes. "[They] are converted, 'so to speak, to culture.' Certainly something of this kind happened to me at Columbia."[37]

The proportion of Jewish undergraduates at Ivy League colleges more than doubled between 1945 and the 1980s—from 10 percent or less at most Ivies to roughly 25 percent. In the same period, Jews went from unwelcome or (at best) interesting oddities in Ivy League culture to ordinary, full-throated participants.

Before the reform, Jews, Catholics and blacks were scarce among teachers as well as students at prestigious private colleges. In 1930, four full professors out of Yale's 158 total were Jews—making 2.5 percent, ironically not far from the proportion of Jews in the population as a whole, but way beneath the proportion of qualified Jews. ("Qualified Jews" are nearly always a drug on the market.) None of these four were professors in Yale College, the sacred core of the institution. These scarce and exotic Jewish professors taught law or medicine, or taught science at the Sheffield Scientific School— then separate, but now absorbed into Yale proper.

The absence of Jewish professors at Yale College emphasizes the fundamentally social versus intellectual mission of the elite schools before reformation. Becoming a gentleman did not require studying medicine or law or science. It hinged on character. Insofar as classwork had anything to do with it, the history and literature of Anglo-American civilization mattered most.

In 1946, Yale was down to zero Jewish full professors. But in 1960, 11 percent of the faculty were Jews; the reform was making itself felt even at the most reactionary institutions.

The big break for Jews in the upper reaches of the academic elite came in 1968 when Edward Levi, grandson of a rabbi, became president of the University of Chicago. Other major colleges—MIT, the University of Michigan, Caltech—soon acquired Jewish presidents of their own. The Ivy League was breached in due course: Harold Shapiro became president of Princeton in 1988, Neil Rudenstine (father Jewish, mother of Italian descent) president of Harvard in 1991, Richard Levin head of Yale in 1993.

Watching the sustained expansion in the number of Jews as students, then faculty, then deans and presidents of the leading universities means watching intellectual excellence unseat social prominence as the grand organizing principle. Jews had argued for intellectual merit as the decisive criterion in college admissions and hiring and promotion. Not the only criterion—colleges would continue to favor children of alumni, athletes, and so forth; but Jews were more than satisfied with intellectual merit as the *main* criterion.

Once the door was open to Jews, the seal was punctured; purity was lost. What was the point of maintaining the exclusivity of an institution that was full of Jews? That old WASP exclusivity withdrew like an irritated tortoise into the innermost niches of society.

Of course, Jews were eager and aggressive proponents of civil rights for blacks. As soon as they were ensconced at some institution, they were apt to speak up for civil rights. Tom Wolfe cites the sociologist Seymour Martin Lipset: "The integrationist movement was largely an alliance between Negroes and Jews (who, to a considerable extent, actually dominated it). Many of the interracial civil-rights organizations have been led and financed by whites, and the majority of their white members have been Jews."[38]

This grand alliance fell apart in the second half of the 1960s. The Black Power contingent, as opposed to the obsolete and repudiated integrationists for whom Dr. King spoke, saw Jews as the shop-owning, landlording, small-capitalist exploiters of poor blacks in the urban slums. At least, they professed to see them that way. But Jew-hatred has universal appeal. No anti-Semite has ever needed an excuse—or been caught short when asked to invent one.

The move to merit-driven decision making had been promoted as a remedy to anti-Jewish bigotry. It did not mean the automatic elimination of bigotry against blacks, or against women, but it made any sort of bigotry increasingly untenable.

Pure merit was the decisive criterion at many elite college admissions offices from the mid-1950s through the mid-1970s, when affirmative action started to bite. The miracle is not that merit died so young but that it lived so long. A college admissions procedure based on merit alone is inherently rare and fleeting, a fast-decaying isotope. The same holds for nearly any selection process driven by merit.

The rise of affirmative action began with Richard Nixon's executive order (the "Philadelphia Order") of 1969, insisting on an active search for qualified blacks and not merely a passive end to antiblack bigotry in Philadelphia's unionized construction trades. No one ever suggested that top universities must search out qualified Jews; crowds of such Jews were hammering at the doors. Jews never sought any sort of Jewish preference. They argued that all candidates should be judged the same way—which required, in effect, that universities turn themselves into meritocracies.

But meritocracy can't last. Those who don't make the grade will always see unfairness in the very definition of "the grade." Before the Great Reform, elite private colleges discriminated against Jews, Catholics and blacks, in favor of WASPs. Today they discriminate against white Jews, white Catholics and white Protestants, in favor of blacks and other minorities, and often against men and in favor of women.

There is a rough analogy between Jews and blacks, but none at all between Jews and women or blacks and women. Throughout history, many men have been closer to a woman (mother, wife, daughter) than to anyone else in their lives. This doesn't change the fact of prejudice against women, but suggests a story that is no ordinary battle over bigotry.

Consider two Cynthia Ozick pieces twelve years apart.[39] The first (1965) shows us the shame of the old ways. Society, male and female, kept women out casually, carelessly, with a shrug and a chuckle. Opponents who laugh in your face are among the hardest to fight. "No one has been serious and passionate, and certainly no one has been argumentative," she wrote, "concerning attitudes about women. The rebels are few." The second piece (1977) argues that feminism has already gone too far and missed the mark when it insisted that "women writers" are a class of their own. The whole point of feminism had been to fling open the gates and let women join the regular humans. Evaluating both pieces later, in 1983, Ozick wrote, "I found that the new exclusions and psychological definitions of the shapers of this [feminist] movement exactly matched the old exclusions and definitions. A politics of sex had come into being to undermine classical feminism."

In 1965, at the start of modern feminism, women had already succeeded in many fields, especially the arts. Every area covered by universities was open to them—business, law and the hard sciences included. But many women had to push forward through thick, spiny groves of prejudice on their way to advanced degrees or careers, and they often came out stung and bloodied. The law played women and men differently, sometimes favoring women (in custody fights after divorce) but more often men.

Modern feminism has changed all that. Women are welcome in every academic field and nearly all nonacademic ones. It would have been a fine success had left-liberal interventionism stopped there. It didn't.

Affirmative action is the greatest prejudice creator ever devised. No segregationist or misogynist could have done better: affirmative action, in effect, dresses women up in loud clothing labeled "I had it easy" in huge letters, front and back. Naturally, organizations that are hot to recruit women tend to have lower standards for their female recruits. When men *and* women meet a newly recruited female, wondering about her fitness is merely rational. For males, resenting the red-carpet, brass-band, keys-to-the-city treatment that welcomes new females is only human. And this sacred affirmative action drama, still enacted regularly at a college near you, has become a theater of the absurd—because each of the young men and women players grew up in a society where *the only* sex-based prejudice they ever knew was affirmative action prejudice, *against men*. No Beckett or Pirandello could have done better.

———

The welcoming of blacks and women into the elite were two of the most important consequences of the Great Reform. But the reform wasn't per se this changing mix of flavors in the exquisite bouquet of elite academia. It was a change in attitude. That change caused the end of bigotry—and was furthered, in turn, by the new types who arrived *because* bigotry had ended. The change was a redefinition of the term "elite," from a social elite to an ostensibly intellectual one, and the replacement of old WASP attitudes by the intelligentsia's ideas. Instead of being ladies and gentlemen in training, students became presumptive intellectuals. Instead of being American citizens in training, they became presumptive citizens of the world.

The Great Reform of the colleges was directly reflected, to some extent, in the informal class structure of the American elite. Before World War II, the upper crust spoke about being "in society": either you were or you weren't, and *society* meant old, rich families and just a few immensely wealthy new ones. But in 1964, Edmund Wilson reported going from one Manhattan party straight to another in the same building, "where everybody was even richer"; at this second party, the guests "seemed to be a mixture of old society (Vanderbilts and Whitneys) with café society—now to some extent, I suppose, the same thing."⁴⁰ By "café society" he meant the showbiz celebrities and hangers-on who once filled Manhattan's glamorous nightclubs.

———

We know the universities changed, but what changed them? What made them seek different students—ambitious as always, but smarter and more aggressive and less WASP than ever before? What made them hire and promote different faculty, choose different leaders? They did so for many reasons.

One simple, important reason is the GI Bill, or the "Servicemen's Readjustment Act," which passed Congress in 1944. It was a large act that included home loans and unemployment insurance for veterans, but its most important sections covered education. The GI Bill supplied full scholarships and stipends to veterans at colleges and training schools. By 1947, veterans were 49 percent of all college admissions. When the program ended in 1956, nearly half the nation's sixteen million World War II veterans had been to college or training school on the GI Bill.

Nothing in the bill directly affected elite college admissions; the nation's schools were free to accept or reject whomever they liked. But *all* veterans qualified under the bill, which made no mention of race or religion. This national act of nondiscriminatory gratitude changed the moral atmosphere. In fact, military service during the war had some effect in itself: so many American men were drafted, so many others enlisted, that soldiers and sailors often found themselves in small, tight-knit groups that included types they'd never consorted with before. James Fahey's *Pacific War Diary, 1942–1945* (1992) gives some fascinating examples involving Jews from Brooklyn who shared his life on a light cruiser that saw repeated heavy action. Irwin Shaw's story "Act of Faith" (1950) is a study of collapsing anti-Semitism in the army.

At the same time, Nazi Germany opened a grand vista from fashionable anti-Semitism straight into the bowels of hell. The nation had never before come to grips with the moral significance of bigotry. Those with a sharp moral sense (E. B. White, for example) had always seen racial and religious bigotry for what it was. But to most people, bigotry had seemed like a purely social matter. You choose your own friends and associates; no free country could possibly regulate such choices. Obviously, people are apt to work and pass time with other people like themselves.

This holds for Jews and blacks as much as anyone else. Choosing students to admit to some school, or candidates to hire, seemed like a social decision on the lines of choosing which people to invite into your club or your house, or which person to marry.

But the war taught the horrific consequences of bigotry—stripped it bare and exposed it as a sin. Thereafter, the nation confronted the moral implications, and with astonishing speed. Within one generation after the war (by 1965), anti-Semitism was all but gone from public life. Within two generations (by 1990), race prejudice was nearly gone.

—————

While barriers to talent were being demolished, other social forces provided further arguments for the intellectualizing of top universities. One was the hugely heightened status of science and medicine in the years following World War II. Another was American society's increasing tendency to seek out experts, specialists, professionals.

Specialization and professionalization had been clear trends since the nineteenth century. The rise of professional sports is one consequence. Amateur athletes often played many sports, but professionals usually stuck to one. Professional hockey, tennis and football were all small-scale operations at the end of World War II; college football and amateur tennis were the main acts. But the scene changed quickly. In general, specialists and experts had to be talented, and usually they had to be smart, or at least be able to fake it.

The growing prestige of science also seemed to argue for meritocracy and the advancement of intellectuals. Science was famous for its dispassionate interest in talent and results wherever they came from. And science was Emerald City: you couldn't go there but you could see it glittering benevolently on its mountaintop. It was the opposite of Kafka's Castle, a vision equally impenetrable, imperturbable, powerful, fascinating, unapproachable; but while the Castle was ominous, Science City was closer to the medieval vision of the Celestial Jerusalem.

In pre–World War II American culture, "scientist" had been an especially eccentric type of intellectual. *Bringing Up Baby* (1938) has Cary Grant—the greatest comedian in movie history—as the perfect absent-minded science professor, innocent to the point of imbecility. He plays a fumbling, nearsighted paleontologist, bossed by his grim fiancée and humanized at last by Katherine Hepburn, in her funniest screen performance.

But Cary was a mere harmless eccentric awaiting reform. In the remarkable *Carefree* (1938), Fred Astaire is a psychiatrist; his hobbies are golf and dancing perfectly. When Ralph Bellamy, a posh lawyer, loses Ginger (who is lovelier than in any other movie) to Astaire the dancing psychiatrist, he denounces Fred to Ginger as *a scientist.* Into this word he has packed a ton of high-explosive contempt. In the prewar era, scientists were smart and probably valuable, but also vaguely frightening and primarily foreign, with German accents (making them, conveniently, either German *or* Jewish). And their researches were wrapped in perfect obscurity. Whether they were in fact doing science in their labs or just playing Scrabble and fooling around would have been impossible for most Americans to tell.

Cary Grant did the absent-minded scientist again after the war in *Monkey Business* (1952). Sid Caesar's recurring "professor" shtick with Carl Reiner, on Caesar's various hit TV series during the 1950s, was usually a goofball idiot-scientist routine. The type gradually disappeared during the 1960s, to be replaced not by the maniac of *Doctor Strangelove*—the 1964 movie that never impressed the public half as much as the intellectuals—but by the heroic "steely-eyed missilemen" of NASA and the space program.

On the other hand, the hero of Sinclair Lewis's widely read novel *Arrowsmith* (1925) is a young doctor dedicated to research. Lewis was assisted in the writing by Paul de Kruif, an American microbiologist who published his own book in 1926, a bestseller about medical and biological research called *Microbe Hunters*. The public was primed to take biology seriously after the big advances in medicine, surgery and public health during the late nineteenth and early twentieth centuries.

Engineers and technologists were already growing fast in public esteem before the war. Thomas Edison died in 1931, Guglielmo Marconi in 1937, Orville Wright not until 1948. Technology probably charged forward faster and changed life more dramatically in the first half of the twentieth century than ever before or since. And new technologies were increasingly apt to be mysterious and impenetrable to the average man; increasingly, technology seemed to demand not just good old American know-how but scientific training and a powerful brain. The technologist was moving out of the garage, washing the grease off his hands, changing his shirt, studying physics, and acquiring a blackboard for the writing of mysterious equations. Anyone could see how a steam engine worked, and the same held for the incandescent lightbulb, a movie camera, even Hoover Dam. Airplanes and internal combustion engines weren't hard to fathom either. Working on cars was a teenage boy's pastime. But radio was another story. The generation, transmission and transformation of electric power were largely mysterious too, and no single development changed everyday life more than the rise of the electric power industry.

Thomas Edison and Henry Ford were first-class, worldwide celebrities before World War II, and stood for the growing power of technology. Albert Einstein was a worldwide superstar at least as big as anyone else on earth, except (perhaps) for Charles Lindbergh. Everyone knew Einstein had transformed physics forever, although almost no one understood how. He was and remains the perfect symbol of sheer intellectual force.

After the war, biology and medicine made vast improvements in everyday life. Alexander Fleming had discovered penicillin in 1928, and it was used successfully in small clinical tests during the 1930s; but it first became widely available after the war. Until the development of penicillin and sulfanilamide drugs, which arrived in the 1930s, there had been no way to treat bacterial infections. A pinprick might become infected and, if so, you might die; people did. In 1955, Jonas Salk developed the first vaccine against polio. Polio was mainly a disease of children. It left people crippled for life, as it did Franklin Roosevelt (although he contracted the disease as an adult).

These and other scientific, medical and technological developments—including the rise of the digital computer during the 1950s—proclaimed the huge power of science; and the power of science was the power of the human intellect. Leading universities naturally sought out scientific talent for their faculties and student bodies. Admission and hiring by merit was the way to get it. That Einstein, Salk and many other famous scientists were Jews underlined the case against academic anti-Semitism. The administrations of Franklin Roosevelt and then John Kennedy imported experts and intellectuals from the universities—mainly economists and other social scientists and scholars—thereby making intellect glamorous. (Power is *nearly* always the Great Glamorizer. Henry Kissinger famously said that power is an aphrodisiac, although somehow it never seemed to work for his boss Richard Nixon.)

Another external factor in the Great Reform: Americans in the generations after the First World War were increasingly cosmopolitan, increasingly prone to be influenced by Europe, where artists and intellectuals were held in higher esteem than in businesslike America. Europe's growing influence on American culture—and America's influence on Europe at the same time—was partly a result of the many servicemen who fought in Europe in the two world wars. Better, cheaper communication and transportation had a lot to do with it; so did movies and audio recordings. George Gershwin wrote *An American in Paris* in 1928, but the movie of that name (with an awkward Leslie Caron and the ever-abrasive

Gene Kelly) opened in 1951, when European touches were even more pervasive in American culture than they had been in the 1920s.

When America's top colleges had been satisfied to admire Oxford and Cambridge, the society university seemed exactly right. But when they decided that Paris was a better bet—the Paris of Sartre, Camus and their fellow existentialists, of Matisse, Picasso, Giacometti and Chagall, of sidewalk cafés and the Left Bank—then the society university was no longer good enough. An intellectuals' university seemed far more chic.

——◦——

One final factor in the takeover of the elite universities, the coup of the intellectuals, is the hardest to pin down; but it was decisive. The WASPs who had founded the great universities, put up their buildings, paid their bills, supplied their art collections, rooted for their football teams, populated their student bodies, faculties and governing councils were just as firmly in control in 1946 as they had ever been. But in 1946, all sorts of trends and forces harried, urged, stung and nagged the Harvards, Yales, Princetons, Columbias forward on the path of reform. In the end, the WASP leaders stepped aside, opened their gates wide and let the intellectuals roar in like a heathen horde for one big reason: they wanted to.

Nearly all revolutions are collaborations between the ins and the outs. The pull created by an elite that is losing the will to fight can be just as powerful as the push of rebels who want in. Vacuums are as potent as forward surges. Sometimes the pull *creates* the rebellion.

The old WASP establishment could have kept control; could at least have fought for control as they were besieged by swarms of stinging, biting, dangerous new ideas. But they stepped aside. They handed over the keys to the city without a fight, or without much of one. It must have felt like entrusting the daughter you have reared and loved to some stranger you barely know who proposes to marry her.

Henry James's *The American* (1877) centers on a wealthy, self-made American businessman (youngish, with quiet but colossal self-assurance) who goes to Paris and falls in love with a girl of rank in the French nobility. They agree to marry, with her family's consent: the family needs money and is willing to stoop for it. But the lady's mother and brother step in at the last moment to prevent the marriage, and the lady, rather than marry the nobleman they have chosen for her on the spur of the moment, consigns herself to a convent forever. The American suffers, and finally arrives at the means to get even, to destroy the reputation of the arrogant aristocrats who have ruined his happiness, by revealing a dark secret of their past. He is ready to do it. And yet—and yet—he doesn't. He just goes away.

The French noblemen knew he would. They understood the reality of rock-solid American decency. They knew the heft and tone and ring of real nobility when they saw and heard it. They had none themselves, but they knew the American had plenty of the genuine article.

That solid decency was the decisive factor. It made the WASPs open the gates and get out of the way. Despite Norman Mailer's being the type of the left-wing artist-intellectual, he penetrates to the truth nearly as often as he talks nonsense. (Sometimes vicious nonsense.) He writes in *Miami and the Siege of Chicago* (1968) about Republican delegates and their families arriving for the presidential convention that nominated Richard Nixon. Here, he says,

> was the muted tragedy of the Wasp—they were not on
> earth to enjoy or even perhaps to love so very much,
> they were here to serve. . . . And so much of America
> did not wish them to serve any longer, and so many

of them doubted themselves, doubted that the force of their faith could illumine their path in these new modern horror-head times.[41]

Forget the stuff about love and enjoyment; the core of this paragraph is true.

chapter four

Imperial Academia

WHILE REFORM CHANGED THE CHARACTER OF AMERICAN UNIVERSITIES, they were slurping over the brim of their ivy-covered containers like overleavened dough in some old Bugs Bunny cartoon, and reaching deeper and deeper into every corner of American culture.

The biggest factor in the increased power and reach of elite universities: far more Americans go to college now than in 1940. Only a small portion attend elite colleges, but the elite colleges strongly influence the rest. In 1940, about 5 percent of American adult men and 3 percent of women had finished four years of college. Today that figure is about 30 percent, for men and women. The strongest growth happened in the two generations after the war, between 1946 and 1990. George Schmidt's *The Liberal Arts College* reported in 1957 that "most pressing and immediate among the problems confronting colleges and universities today are those caused by their rapid growth. An unprecedented number of students are thronging our institutions of higher education, and, barring catastrophes, this number is almost certain to increase at an accelerated rate for years to come."[1] And so it did.

Far more Americans are finishing high school also. In 1940, less than a quarter of American adults, men and women, had finished four years of high school. By 1990, three-quarters had. Today it's roughly 80 percent. Of course, the cultural revolution has changed the nature of high school (not just college) education in all sorts of ways.

A glance at the old world: the wryly funny *Father of the Bride* was a hit in 1950, with Spencer Tracy, Joan Bennett and a young Elizabeth Taylor. Spencer is a partner in a law firm, a grade-A block of upper-middle-class WASP granite. But his wife, who is just as respectable as Spencer in every particular, never finished high school. They were married when she was seventeen; and—she points out to her husband—while the rest of her high school class graduated with due ceremony, she was in the hospital having a baby. Although such practices were not standard among the upper-middle WASPhood, neither did they raise eyebrows.

Another element in the huge blossoming of academic influence and power was the growing entourage that faculties began to accumulate after World War II, as if they were prizefighters or aircraft carriers. Columbia University's budget increased from $20 million to $120 million between 1953 and 1966; only one-sixth of that was inflation. Yet the number of students remained the same.

The expansion partly reflected new organizations within the university: "centers, programs, institutes, research projects, exchange agreements, partnerships and affiliations," writes Jacques Barzun, who was dean of faculty and then provost (and also a distinguished thinker). Furthermore, by the end of the 1950s the senior faculty were being replaced two for one. "For every senior scholar who retired or resigned, the regular departments of instruction found themselves requiring two new men of high repute and costly qualifications." Why? Because of the "rapid splitting up of subject matters into new specialties" (a process that sounds suspiciously like a nuclear chain reaction), and because of all those new "centers, programs, institutes," and so forth.[2]

The whole institution of American education is a megaphone to amplify the musings of elite universities. As more and more people, a growing fraction of a growing American population, climbed inside this elite clown-car—all those top universities together—the top-drawer colleges gained steadily in influence. At the same time, their professional and graduate schools were becoming more influential; and in this way, too, the top colleges deepened the impression they were stamping on American culture.

One of the important ways in which leading universities wield influence is through their education schools, which send forth a new group of fresh-faced young evangelists on their mission-to-the-Gentiles every year. Not all top universities have them, but Harvard's is always among the top-ranked, and so are Stanford's, and Columbia's Teachers College. Berkeley, the University of Michigan, Johns Hopkins, UCLA and the University of Pennsylvania are other top universities with leading education schools.

Back in 1917, the "man in the Brooks Brothers shirt" in Mary McCarthy's story was a "chemistry major, just out of state university, with a job for the next year teaching science at a high school."[3] To prepare to teach some topic, in private or public school, you mastered that topic. Education courses—not to mention ed-school degrees—were strictly optional. Only in the years following World War II did a BA become a nearly universal requirement for elementary school teachers, but education schools had been growing since the founding of Teachers College at Columbia in 1887. A common path to teaching used to be the generic "teachers' colleges," designed to take high school graduates and make teachers out of them. Mostly these colleges turned into undergraduate or graduate education schools or departments, or in some cases full-blown universities in their own right.

In the first decades of the twentieth century, ed-school faculties came to dominate the national discussion of education, displacing liberal arts faculties as education became a field in itself. After World War II, the trend toward specialization and professionalization further increased the advantage held by "educationists" over other academics in discussing schools and school reform. (An axiom about schools: however they're doing, they need reforming.) The ever-growing influence of education schools was the topic of James Conant's widely discussed *Education of American Teachers* (1963). Conant was a respected "educationist" himself, but his book argued that advanced ed-school degrees and even undergraduate education courses were unnecessary in making a teacher; a supervised stint of student teaching and college training in the subject matter to be taught—not how but *what* to teach—were the only steps guaranteed to pay off.

Naturally, Conant's book changed nothing. Education schools were temporarily ticked off, but continued to wield a large and increasing influence, and teachers' associations continued to carry their point: education was a full-blown profession, just like medicine or law. No, scratch law. Just like medicine, dammit! Or *surgery!* So while the Harvards and Stanfords and Columbias were changing, and their education schools changed along with them, the scope and influence of the top universities continued to grow.

———

Business schools followed a similar path. This time, Harvard was the hero. The Harvard Business School, founded in 1908, became the first school in history to grant MBA degrees. Hurrah! But in the years before World War II, business schools were in their childhood and the term itself was ambiguous. Kay is one of Mary McCarthy's heroines in *The Group* (1963); at the time she marries (in the 1930s), she has "already registered for a typing course in business school."[4] So much for your fancy MBAs.

Harvard Business School's history is a synopsis of business school history in general. Business schools want to keep students a full two years and send them forth with MBAs. Before the war, only half of Harvard's students finished the two-year degree program; but by 1948—after a flood of postwar applications—the figure was nearly 100 percent. Applications kept increasing, and so did the number of companies that came calling at Harvard to do job interviews. The growing prominence of business schools generated controversy during the 1950s (as the ed schools had also done): does an MBA do an aspiring businessman any good in itself, or is business school just a matter of meeting people and getting yourself stamped with the highest-prestige seal of approval you can manage? That controversy continues today, but the answer doesn't matter; either way, the elite business schools exercise a large influence and magnify the importance of their universities.

In 1957, at any rate, several negative reports on the MBA—attacking it as a third-rate vocational program—bothered Harvard into making changes and introducing a modern-style program: required courses in the first year, specialization in the second. The 1960s were years of flat-out growth. By the early '70s, Harvard Business School was winded, and growth slowed. But the business schools had already arrived as major shaping influences in American culture.

———

Columbia University was the leader once again in the emergence of journalism schools. Columbia's was founded in 1912, to offer journalism classes to students throughout the university. In 1935 it became America's first graduate school of journalism.

But look around in 1940, when many leading writers and reporters didn't even have BAs, much less journalism degrees. Take some of the star foreign correspondents of the Second World War: Ernie Pyle (the most popular), A. J. Liebling (often called the best), the broadcasting pioneers Edward R. Murrow and William Shirer, and John Hersey, who wrote the famous *New Yorker* issue devoted entirely to Hiroshima. Pyle and Liebling never finished college. Murrow, Shirer and Hersey finished their BA degrees and hired out as reporters. Of the five, only Liebling graduated from journalism school, at Columbia—although he had no BA. Harold Ross, the remarkable editor and reporter who founded the *New Yorker* and edited every issue from the first in 1925 until his death in 1951, dropped out of school at thirteen.

In the postwar years, Columbia Journalism School grew predictably in influence, and the 1960s saw expansion and the development of a curriculum that is still standard today. In 1961, the *Columbia Journalism Review* was founded—a big step toward bringing journalism into the academic fold and granting it diplomatic recognition, so to speak.

Journalism schools have been controversial the same way education and business schools have. *Who the hell needs them?* (To compress one side of the argument somewhat.) Is journalism—or writing itself—an academic field like history or chemistry? Or might it be a learn-by-doing skill, like gardening or auto mechanics? Naturally the universities wanted to convert as much of the landscape as possible into fenced-off, neatly tended, carefully patrolled academic preserves. *Keep off the grass.* And the nation as a whole had a generous impulse (still does) to push people upscale—socially, economically, academically. But is journalism school in fact good preparation for a career in journalism? No one who is disinterested seems to know.

Teacher's Pet, a 1958 movie with Clark Gable and Doris Day, is valuable as a plain statement of the theory that (1) nearly everyone needs a college degree and (2) professionalization is the royal road to a secure and sophisticated future. To be just like medicine is, again, the aspiration of every trade and profession. (In

1958, doctors are highly respected, highly trained, decently paid and sometimes able to make sick people better. It wasn't always that way!) To be just like *science*, on the other hand, is the goal of the social sciences—hot topics in the postwar academic economy.

Obviously, Hollywood movies show film-set fantasies of American life, not reality. But Hollywood is exquisitely sensitive, a pathologically high-strung racehorse aware of every thought and fancy of its various jockeys—especially its establishment jockeys, who write the reviews and pass the word.

In *Teacher's Pet,* Doris Day is charming, if (as usual) not quite equal to the femme fatale demands of her role. Gable does his gruff, hard-drinking, womanizing but deep-down kindly role with mesmerizing low-key authority. But the film is also a billboard for the benefits of college education and professionalization, erected at a point on the highway where America was still not 100 percent sold on either.

The movie follows a boy just out of high school who wants to be a reporter, and the city editor of a big New York paper (Gable) who takes him on as errand boy and apprentice. The boy's mother is desperate for him to quit the paper and go to college. Apprenticing, learning on the job—with maybe some vocational school training along the way—was the old route to learning a trade. Going to college was the new route.

Gruff Gable has been asked to give a talk at Columbia Journalism School. He refuses, because he thinks journalism school is nonsense. And he refuses the mother's entreaty to fire her boy and let him go to college, because he thinks college is nonsense too. He seethes with contempt for the "college boys" who work for him; he never finished high school, while they've got BA degrees, even a Phi Beta Kappa key in one case—and are nonetheless mere menials in his service. This contemptuous phrase *college boys,* with an ominous rolling growl, was a motif in postwar movies. Jimmy Cagney does the growl with more sheer menace than anyone else, in *Mister Roberts* (1955), where he's the noncollege boy in command of a rear-echelon Navy supply ship during the war. He depends on the unfailing competence of his right-hand man Henry Fonda, *college boy,* who wants desperately to be reassigned to a combat ship but can't be so long as Cagney vetoes his transfer requests. And Cagney vetoes them again and again, partly because he depends on Fonda and knows it, mainly because he hates his guts. In fact, he hates all *college boys.* Cagney gets his in the end.

Meanwhile, back at *Teacher's Pet*—the journalism school professor who invited Gable to lecture turns out to be Doris Day, who sticks to her guns. She insists to her class (voice quivering with emotion) that journalism is a *profession,* not a mere trade, and that sending young people into journalism without adequate training in journalism school is just like . . . well, like . . . yes! Like allowing untrained people to pass as doctors! Professional school degrees don't summon up many emotional outbursts or dramatic speeches anymore, but these were serious open questions in the postwar generation.

This is what the professionalization of America was supposed to be all about: a forward-thinking, rocket-engined faith in the power of colleges and graduate schools to exalt American society up, up, up into the stratosphere of a glorious future, in contrast to the burnt-out Model T idea of pushing people from high school straight into work or marriage, where they learn on the job. This belief in the saving power of college and university education was by no means restricted to academics; it was so widespread that Doris Day got to embody it in a Hollywood movie. And this new faith in colleges and graduate and professional schools was promoted with the straightforward, plainspoken passion that only America can bring to this sort of argument.

The argument continues today. The college-educated proportion of America continues to creep upward. The groundwork was laid in the postwar generation, the *Teacher's Pet* era.

Along the way, the movie sticks up for the social sciences also. They too were expanding rapidly in the 1950s, and trying hard to be taken seriously. Gig Young plays a brilliant psychology professor who knows how to do the samba, a popular dance of demented complexity. At the start, Gable can't say the word "psychologist" without a heavy sneer. But Gig opens his eyes. In the end, Gable comes around: sends the boy off to college, acknowledges the importance of journalism school, concedes that newspapers and the world are changing, and takes Doris away from Gig. Henceforth, he admits, reporters will have to think harder, dig deeper, get more educated.

Doris's character makes one last fascinating point. People don't need newspapers to tell them the news anymore; it's *1958!* People get breaking news around-the-clock on radio or television. Newspapers need something *new* to do. (Call us when they find it.)

The growing cult of the expert is also on view in *The Dick Van Dyke Show,* a half-hour comedy that ran on CBS from fall 1961 through spring '66. Unlike *Teacher's Pet*, it was a milestone: one of the best-written, best-acted shows in TV history. It's still funny fifty years later—after you've retuned from today's blazingly vulgar comedies for the concentration-span-challenged to the lower-key, smarter, more sophisticated style of the early 1960s.

Dick Van Dyck and Mary Tyler Moore are a young couple, he a comedy writer for a hit TV show and she a former dancer turned wife and mother. He's graceful, elegant, charming; she is too, and also beautiful. They live in a Manhattan suburb. This is the center of the action in Classic America, 1960–65. Those years were the gorgeous, glamorous height of American civilization—at least so far. Those were our Periclean years.

What did an educated, suburban, middle-class young couple do with itself in those years of grace, when most of the country felt good and resolved to be better all the time? When people cared about the arts, science, world affairs? Our young couple goes to the theater often; these were the last great days of Broadway, but Dick and Mary ("Mr. and Mrs. Robert Petrie") also go off-Broadway to see avant-garde productions. They see lots of movies, including foreign ones (notably Swedish); they have guests who chat about Ingmar Bergman, a 1960s favorite. When the topic turns to the public-spirited doctor and former organist Albert Schweitzer, Dick sits down at the piano and plays a snippet of Bach—the audience being expected to know that it is Bach, and that Schweitzer was famous for performing Bach. Sometimes Dick and Mary sing and soft-shoe as a couple, with casual, devastating charm: no couple has ever done it better, with such flawless musicianship and taste and grace. They visit Manhattan art galleries routinely, decorate their living room with tastefully framed reproduction Picassos, watch ballet on television, and might or might not be reading Thomas Mann's *Magic Mountain* (another '60s vogue); at any rate, they have a copy in their living room. And mainly, of course, they think about sex.

There's a fascinating reflection in a pair of episodes, in seasons two and four, of developing American ideas about expertise and professionalization. The two episodes have nearly the same plot: a child in elementary school is caught using obscenities or sounding off about sex in school. What will the parents do? In season two ('62–'63) they learn how to deal with the problem, "in an atmo-sphere of mutual love and understanding," from a minister and his wife. But in season four ('64–'65), the world has leapt forward and ministers are passé. This time, the parents learn wisdom from the school psychiatrist. In fact, they are warned not to discuss the topic with their son until they have visited the school for "professional guidance." To the father, this idea is absurd; he can't talk to his own boy without "professional guidance"? But wait!—patient, lovable Mom restrains him. And so they wait for professional wisdom; for the smooth, manicured green lawn of science to replace the wild sweet meadow-grass of common sense.

Robert McNamara was running the Vietnam War on the same principle. His dispassionate scientific analysis turned the wisdom and experience of mere military officers into outmoded irrelevancies.

Dick Van Dyke episodes like the visit to the school psychiatrist were gently satirical and funny. But they were also part of a broad cultural trend that set out to make *professional guidance* spoken contemptuously by fathers sound as silly as *college boys* spoken contemptuously by undereducated city editors and naval officers. Unfortunately, there *was* a certain wisdom in all that anti-intellectual prejudice, envy and bile. American society will always need and depend on noncollege boys, assuming that people will still drive trucks and buses, build and fix things, put out fires and police the streets. The idea that everyone needs a college education was always silly. That nearly everyone should then proceed from college to graduate school is even sillier.

Graduate and professional degree programs of all sorts have grown enormously since 1946, in numbers and prominence. We can trace the increasing size of the programs, but it's hard to pin down their increasing influence—although we are all aware of it.

Consider the U.S. presidency since 1946. Neither Harry Truman nor Dwight Eisenhower nor John Kennedy nor Lyndon Johnson had a graduate degree. Truman, in fact, was the first president since the nineteenth century without a bachelor's degree—and he might be the last forever. But five of the eight presidents *since* Johnson did have advanced degrees: Nixon, Ford, Clinton and Obama from law school, George W. Bush from Harvard Business School.

The large influence of the elite universities continues to grow. Before the cultural revolution, Hollywood and the old Eastern universities, for example, were largely nonintersecting elites. The film studios had East Coast offices where Ivy Leaguers (lawyers especially) were sometimes to be found, but Hollywood itself was run by self-made men, many of them Jews, who had improvised a new industry from scratch in a faraway, sunny nowhere. An occasional Princeton-educated writer might go west seeking to cash in. But Scott Fitzgerald explains in *The Love of the Last Tycoon,* his unfinished last novel, why he at least didn't make it as a screen-writer: storytelling in the movies is a new animal, dependent on quick, powerful connections between picture and emotion. The hero of the *Last Tycoon,* based on the legendary producer Irving Thalberg, is a new kind of industrial giant and a new kind of artist. He owes nothing to the old WASP elite.

But look at "Yale in Hollywood" today. It's a branch of the Yale Alumni Society that runs its own meetings and special events. Read its list of Yale alums in the film industry and it's clear that Yale today is all over Hollywood—and likewise Princeton, Harvard, Berkeley, Chicago et al. Among the Yale graduates are actors and actresses, writers and all sorts of producers, heads of marketing and publicity companies, film-industry investors, movie-music composers, licensing-company executives, agents and (of course) Hollywood lawyers.

Welcome to American culture, where—now more than ever—the tony universities are the ultimate source of attitude.

chapter five

The Road to the Late '60s

DURING THE 1950S, THE PORGIS BEGAN TO FEEL THEIR NEW POWER—BEGAN to light up like switchboards that everyone, suddenly, wants to call. During the 1960s, they occupied the heights and ran their new PORGI flag up the pole. You can watch it climb and snap smartly in the breeze. History helped: President Lyndon Johnson was the perfect smooth rock to step on as the march proceeded. And by the time Nixon took over at the start of 1969, the old American establishment had been reduced to stark raving, roaring, churning chaos, like the sea when the twin screws of some huge ship have started to swirl. When the nation began to settle down again—with the disgrace of Watergate behind it, with American involvement in Vietnam abruptly ended as Congress kicked out the supporting struts and the roof caved in, as President Jimmy Carter took over—the old WASP establishment was gone and the PORGIs were in control. And they have been ever since.

Today, many high school and college students are taught that the 1950s were shabby, cringing years, with Senator Joe McCarthy lording it over the cowering nation like a two-bit Himmler building an American Gestapo. McCarthy was indeed dangerous—and this "cringing America" theory is nonsense. Americans don't like to cringe. In fact, the '50s were brave, confident years, partly because America had won World War II, had beat off loathsome, vicious, mighty enemies to the west and the east— and then, for an encore, managed to rescue South Korea from a Chinese-supported North Korean invasion.

The writer and critic Anatole Broyard writes about New York in 1946: "The war was over, the Depression had ended, and everyone was discovering life's simple pleasures. . . . New York City had never been so attractive. The postwar years were like a great smile in its sullen history. . . . Rents were cheap, restaurants were cheap, and it seemed to me that happiness itself might be cheaply had."[1] A foreign visitor in Randall Jarrell's *Pictures from an Institution* (1954) says, "Here in your country, Art and Commerce and Life are a bitter—no, a sweet pill covered over with sex; if Moses had lived among you he would have returned to find you worshipping not a Golden Calf but a Golden Girl."[2] Evidently the nation's mind was not completely monopolized by McCarthyism. In 1953, Marilyn Monroe was a smash in *Gentlemen Prefer Blondes,* where she sang "Diamonds Are a Girl's Best Friend." In late spring of 1954, Joe McCarthy hit the skids in the Army-McCarthy hearings, and before long he was finished.

America was properly proud of itself, and the economy was booming. I have mentioned William DeVane's view in 1957; it is a genial WASP view, with a touch of Franz Hals—the great, hearty, red-cheeked, pipe-smoking, reassuring elder statesman. Here is DeVane again:

> Our national leaders for the most part are men of
> integrity, idealism, and skill; our literary and artistic
> people command an international respect such as

they never had before; our scientists and engineers,
especially the latter, are the wonder and envy of other
nations; our teachers in our colleges and universities
are learned and devoted.

The nation was comfortable with itself: the civil rights struggle
was under way, but things were good nonetheless. The nation
was willing to admit not merely to being powerful but to being
admirable.

The 1950s were exciting, euphoria-generating years in the
United States, and intellectuals partied alongside everyone else.
Among intellectuals, the party mood had another source too: early
victories in the cultural revolution. Intellectuals were breaking
out of their narrow urban strongholds and storming the heady
heights of American culture. In Wordsworth's famous lines about
the first years of the French Revolution, "Bliss was it in that dawn
to be alive / But to be young was very heaven!" Norman Podhoretz
described the first half of the '50s in *Making It* (1967, before the
change of heart that turned him from radical-left to neoconservative): "The main element of those years—years which were later
to be lumped vulgarly and indiscriminately with the latter part of
the decade as the dull fifties—was an exhilaration at the sudden
and overwhelming appearance of new possibilities, in life as in
consciousness."[3]

These were crucial years for the revolution; and they were
strange years for the American left. Much of the left had decided
to like America or even love it, and to despise Marxism and the
brutal Soviet police state. But this was only a temporary break
in regular service. Radicalism and anti-Americanism resumed,
rested and refreshed, in the 1960s.

—·—

The "Port Huron Statement" of 1962 announced the emergence
of the left-wing Students for a Democratic Society, or SDS, later a

leading mover in the war against the war. The statement begins, "We are people of this generation, bred in at least modest comfort, housed now in universities . . . ." Naturally, *in universities.* Universities would be the center of the action in the social upheaval that was looking for a reason-to-be long before this nation had ever heard of Vietnam.

The student strike at Berkeley during the 1964–65 academic year, led by a radical group called the Free Speech Movement, was another peal of the same big bell, calling the nation to render homage to the new PORGI aristocracy and its taste for Outrage, Alienation and Nihilism. Berkeley students were protesting university rules that limited political activity on campus. The strike was covered at length and in sympathetic detail by the intelligentsia's favorite newspapers and magazines.

Consider this sequence: Franklin Roosevelt, Harry Truman, Adlai Stevenson, John Kennedy, Lyndon Johnson. Who sticks out like a big Tex-Mex enchilada that has somehow got loose and is spreading havoc among the petit-fours?

These men were successive leaders of the Democratic Party from 1932 to 1968—years in which Democrats controlled the White House every year except when Eisenhower the war hero was president. FDR was a glamorous and beloved figure. Truman was antiglamorous, but he beat the Republican Dewey when no one thought he would, and eventually became a hero to liberals. Adlai Stevenson was the Democratic nominee for president in 1952 and '56; he lost to Eisenhower both times. But intellectuals worshipped Stevenson, who seemed like a perfect lightweight intellectual—articulate, soft-spoken, humorous, refined, debonairish, balding—to be petted and encouraged. Like Truman, JFK was initially unpopular among intellectuals, but quickly emerged as the American intelligentsia's number-one heartthrob of all time. (Because intellectuals don't see facts very clearly, they are often dreadfully romantic.) And then came Lyndon Johnson: no less a personage, evidently, than the Greek god of vulgarity in the flesh, descended from Olympus to hold barbeques for an awe-struck nation.

Johnson became president when Kennedy was assassinated. He cared about and advanced civil rights far more aggressively than Kennedy ever had. But Johnson had a problem. Edmund Wilson, 1965: "A law should be passed making it impossible for a Texan to be President."[4] Wilson, a thoroughly liberal man, was a bigot when it came to Texas. And he was not alone. In his 1945–1975 volume of the *Oxford History of the United States*, James Patterson writes that Johnson "always seemed desperately eager to make people love him," "had acquired a reputation as a self-aggrandizing wheeler-dealer," and was widely seen as "a virtual caricature of all that they associated with Texas. Many, noting his shiny, wide-lapelled suits and slicked-back hair, likened him to a riverboat gambler."[5] *Did* many? I doubt it. But Johnson did strike most intellectuals as a thick hick. Hannah Arendt, in a 1965 letter: "He thinks in terms of prestige only, does not know how else to think. Is terribly ambitious and very impatient with disagreement of any kind. Also, quite primitive."[6]

Quite primitive. He spoke with a broad Texas accent (like George W. Bush). He was no intellectual and didn't know how to flatter intellectuals. He was unrefined, not witty, not especially articulate; he was unapologetic about his love of politics and Texas and America and life in general. And the black and bitter contrast between Johnson and his predecessors made it all ter-ribly much worse. Intellectuals couldn't stand him. They hated Johnson fiercely, with their gorges rising in disgust. They hated him even more than they came to hate George W. Bush. (Well, maybe.) Their Johnson-hatred didn't *make* the cultural revolution, or the antiwar movement—but it helped.

Norman Podhoretz had a four-hour talk with Lyndon Johnson— mainly a monologue by Johnson, evidently—at the height of LBJ's power and self-confidence, soon after he'd beaten Barry Goldwater by a landslide; at a time when he'd got the epochal Civil Rights Act of 1964 passed and had launched his "War on Poverty" and other parts of his "Great Society." Johnson's legislative program was a daring attempt to make the federal government swoop down like a falcon on poverty and bigotry, grab one in each powerful claw and destroy them both. Even if one dislikes the idea of the government as a powerful, well-funded raptor, even if one concedes that Johnson's conduct of the war in Vietnam was catastrophically bad (until Abrams replaced Westmoreland in command of American forces), it's impossible to deny the man's nobility, or the majesty of his worldview. Podhoretz found Johnson "extraordinarily intelligent."[7]

Among all American presidents it is, ironically, Johnson rather than Kennedy who comes closest to the type of the tragic hero. Of course, Nixon's presidency was also a tragedy, in a different way; Kennedy's too. This strangely ill-fated passage in American political history, Kennedy-Johnson-Nixon, would make a compelling topic if the establishment didn't still hate Johnson and (especially) Nixon too much to see straight.

In April 1965, Hannah Arendt commented in a letter on President Johnson and the expanding Vietnam War: "I have no confidence in Johnson. . . . The academic community is almost unanimously against him. The people at large are quite apathetic . . . ; no one cares outside the Universities."[8] But the universities would lead the way.

During the summer of 1967, the *New York Review of Books* published on its cover a diagram showing how to make the flame grenade called a Molotov cocktail—the message being that left-liberals who wanted to remake American society should take to the streets and throw bombs. Make them, throw them, and the hell with it. If people burn, they burn. What's important anyway, mere human beings or the Big Idea? The Movement? The Revolution? *Also sprach* the left. Back in the 1930s, the malevolent ravings of left-wing intellectuals had been unimportant to American culture at large. But now, times were different. The colleges were listening (although even the radical left-liberal college students of the late 1960s rarely resorted to Molotov cocktails—despite being grateful, no doubt, for the *Review*'s helpful advice).

chapter six

Snapshot 1968: War, the Elite and the Thinkers

HERE WE ARE AT THE END OF THE CULTURAL REVOLUTION, AND THE BEGIN-ning of its effects on the nation and the world, as it digs its roots into the soil and starts to grow—as the new establishment get into their robes and take their exalted seats.

In October 1967 there was an enormous antiwar march to the Pentagon in Washington. A large crowd piled up in front of the Lincoln Memorial and then tramped across the short bridge into Virginia and down the road to the Pentagon. College students were a driving force in the antiwar movement, and prominent intellectuals took the lead. Norman Mailer describes the march in *The Armies of the Night* (1968).[1] Mailer himself was one of the celebrity intellectuals (Robert Lowell was another) who marched in the front ranks, hoping to be arrested during their rush on the Pentagon to protest America's fight on behalf of South Vietnam. As Norman Podhoretz points out, these so-called antiwar pro-testers "were not against the war at all but only against one of the two sides fighting it." They wanted the Communist North to win.

In *The Inheritance* (1996), Samuel Freedman writes from the other side of the lines.[2] During World War II, Yale men had worked together with normal Americans who were not students at posh colleges: the college men as officers, the others typically as enlisted men. In combat, enlisted men and company officers—lieutenants and captains—lived and fought together on the front lines. But now it was 1967. College men ordinarily had draft deferments, and at the Pentagon march they flaunted them. Yale men and draftees came face to face on opposite sides, the Yale men protesting America's war in Vietnam, the draftees doing their duty as army infantry or military police guarding the Pentagon from the massed protesters. Freedman writes about the peace-marchers "clad in tweed coats and flannel shirts and penny loafers"—that's how college students used to dress in the fall. "Each group bore aloft its sign—'Princeton Seminary,' 'Ethical Culture School,' 'Rutgers Newark,' 'B.U.S.D.S.'" (the Boston University chapter of Students for a Democratic Society). This was the antiwar movement.

Freedman also writes about Tim Carey, who had been drafted into the military police and assigned to keep peace-marchers out of the building that October day. "Hardly anyone in his unit, now that he thought about it, had a college education. Even the officers corps, without enough degreed men from which to draw, were accepting high school graduates."

As the marchers arrived and began operations, intending to provoke the soldiers into starting a fight that would look bad on world TV, a few of the peace-marching women stuck flowers stagily into rifle barrels. Some of the men waved their burning draft cards overhead. Others threw insults and unopened soup cans. "Anyone who had bothered to lug a case of canned soup a mile and a half from the Lincoln Memorial to the Pentagon, Tim realized, had arrived with assault in mind." Trust American college boys to find prepackaged artificial rocks that were just right for hurling: dangerous, and reasonably priced too!

Freedman: [Tim Carey's] training forbade any
   response. He stood rigid as rocks and soda bottles
   fell in squalls, as faces pressed so close to his
   own he could feel the breath. . . . "You're an ass-
   hole. . . . Come on over with us. . . . Do you know
   what you stand for? . . . Just lay down your gun."

Mailer, writing about himself in the third person: He
   headed across the grass to the nearest MP he saw.
   It was as if the air had changed, or light had altered;
   he felt immediately much more alive . . . .

Freedman: Some flew the Viet Cong colors. A placard
   proclaimed, "Avenge Che!" "Johnson Bullshit,"
   offered another. . . . From the stage, one performer
   led a sing-along. . . . "It takes a real man to say, I
   won't go. . . . It takes a real man to say, No."

The cultural revolution had blasted a Grand Canyon between
the college elite and the rest of the country. Even if Vietnam and
not World War II had impended in 1940—and to some left-lib
intellectuals, recall, World War II *was* Vietnam, was *not* worth
fighting, was none of America's damned business!—it's incon-
ceivable that men from Yale or Harvard or Princeton in 1940
would have thrown bottles and rocks and soup cans and insults
at their less-lucky countrymen who were drafted into the service.

Which group was less classy, anyway, at that Pentagon
standoff? The Yale men with their burning draft cards, their rocks
and bottles and soup cans, or the military police trying hard not
to respond to ugly provocation? When MPs stayed and Yale men
ran, who was then the gentleman?

Mailer: To their front was a low rope, not a foot off the
   ground.

Freedman: Those ropes formed part of the scheme for
   avoiding strife . . . .

Mailer: The MP lifted his club to his chest as if to bar
all passage. To Mailer's great surprise—he had
secretly expected the enemy to be calm and strong,
why should they not? . . . —to his great surprise, the
MP was trembling. . . . "Go back," he said hoarsely
to Mailer.

Freedman: "Leave us alone," he ordered fecklessly.
"Get back."

Mailer: As the MP spoke, the raised club quivered.
. . . Was he now possessed of a moral force which
implanted terror in the minds of young soldiers?

Naturally, the MP to whom Mailer refers isn't Tim Carey. But
Carey and Mailer's man were part of the same force on the same
mission on the same day, same time, same place.

Freedman: The goal of the Johnson administration that
day was to "Act in a way which holds to the absolute
minimum the possibility of bloodshed and injury
[and] minimizes the need for arrest," as a planning
memorandum put it.

Mailer: "Listen," said Mailer, "let's get arrested now."

Mailer was addressing a couple of his fellow celebrity-leaders of
the march, Robert Lowell and the essayist Dwight Macdonald,
who had been the real-life model for Mary McCarthy's "Portrait of
the Intellectual as a Yale Man."

Lowell concluded a poem around this time, "Waking Early
Sunday Morning" (1967), with this verse:

Pity the planet, all joy gone
From this sweet volcanic cone;
peace to our children when they fall
in small war on the heels of small
war—until the end of time

to police the earth, a ghost
orbiting forever lost
on our monotonous sublime.

Lowell was preoccupied with his grim left-liberal view of Vietnam and the nation. *All joy gone*—but there was suffering and joy all around him. There was beauty all around, some of it hammered out of red-hot suffering on his own anvil by his own hand. (He was more a jeweler than a blacksmith, though: he made beauty by stringing necklaces out of shimmering iridescent words whose meanings flash out suddenly but only for an instant, like the brilliant deep reds and oranges of a fire opal.)

Mailer's utter lack of moral seriousness and his holiday mood were typical of the peace-marchers. So was his absolute self-absorption. But Mailer was different in one respect: he saw "the enemy" (American soldiers, young draftees) as human beings, or at least tried to. In World War II, Mailer had seen combat himself, against the Japanese. But the bulk of the peace-marcher college students saw things differently. They were soldiers of the cultural revolution, not of the USA.

> *Mailer:* He was arrested, he had succeeded . . . he was in the land of the enemy now, he would get to see their faces.
>
> *Freedman:* Tim Carey finally repaired to his hallway and his sleeping bag. . . . As he relived the experience of the last eight hours, he focused not so much on the soup cans . . . as on a single phrase borne on the wind. . . . Someone was speaking—the comedian Dick Gregory, Tim would later learn—about just who filled the army. "Poor blacks," Tim was pretty sure he had heard, and "dumb whites."

In *Working-Class War* (1993),[3] Christian Appy collects the facts: in Vietnam, 80 percent of American soldiers came from the working classes or the poor. In Harvard's class of 1970 there were 1,200 men, of whom two were veterans.

> *Mailer, on the draft-card-burning event that preceded the Pentagon march:* There seemed to be as many professors and middle-aged faculty present as students, maybe more, and there was an air of Ivy League intimacy to the quiet conversations of this walk—it could not really be called a March.
>
> *Appy:* As the *New York Times* put it, "The typical worker—from construction craftsman to show clerk—has become probably the most reactionary political force in the country."

The new upper classes were no longer wealthy, high-society, conservative WASPs. They were left-wing PORGIs.

Intellectuals and elite college students had conjured up the peace movement. In 1968, opposition to the war became even louder, with student support for Gene McCarthy and Robert Kennedy in the presidential primaries, and the famous battles between peace-marchers and the Chicago police at the Democratic National Convention. Meanwhile, the American public in general remained solidly behind the war effort in Vietnam. Polls showed it; the 1972 landslide re-election of Richard Nixon over the left-wing favorite George McGovern confirmed it. But the intellectuals had captured the establishment, and henceforth *they* were writing the newspapers and history books, and teaching the college courses and ed-school courses. And so Americans today mostly take it for granted that the peace-marchers were right. They take it for granted that it was good we got out of Vietnam, let South Vietnam collapse, and left our friends to face Communist prison camps and executioners alone.

The society college finally died in New Haven on May Day 1970. The body of Alex Rackley, a member of the Black Panthers, had been found floating in a river north of New Haven on April 21, 1969. Rackley had been suspected of being a police informer. Bobby Seale, head of the Panthers, was arrested and charged, along with seven other Panthers. The Panthers and other leading left-liberals announced a mass rally for the accused, to take place in New Haven on May 1, 1970. As the date approached, a Yale faculty meeting suspended "academic expectations" for the rest of the term, meaning that professors could cancel classes; and if they didn't, students could ignore them.

Springtime, the great day approaching: the campus was an armful of daffodils and white-blossoming trees and tentative new leaves and soft grass; and classes abruptly canceled must have made the students slightly drunk. The town girls, and the still-small cohort of Yale coeds, favored miniskirts and microdresses in bright colors, and long, long hair. You'd see the same sort of thing today any mid-Manhattan summer evening—"the girls in their summer dresses" (as in Irwin Shaw's famous short story). Yet it was different back then, because the girls were doing something new with those ultra-short hemlines: edging out on a tightrope, with the special high-strung grace that tightropes impart. They wore light floaty cottony things. In a mild breeze there might be small ripples and billows in the skirts, and those who were standing around chatting might steady the hems with their fingertips. "All life's grandeur / is something with a girl in summer." (Robert Lowell, "Waking Early Sunday Morning," 1967.)

The campus posters were "psychedelic": bright colors mixed with the newly developed fluorescent orange-pinks and yellow-greens, with their strange ugly defiant glow; and students loved to open their windows and set speakers on the ledges pointed outward, so the bump and grind of their rock music could pound the city like a drum. "This is being written in a study in a college of one of the great American universities," George Steiner wrote in *Bluebeard's Castle*; ". . . the walls quiver to the ear or to the touch roughly eighteen hours per day, sometimes twenty-four. The beat is literally unending."[4] Steiner taught at Cambridge and Geneva, but he was visiting Yale. The book appeared in 1971 and would have been written (or finished, anyway) the year before: 1970, Black Panther year. It was not remotely a sweet year or a sweet place; *acid* was one of its favorite words. Shocking brutality seethed under the surface and bubbled up sometimes under the peeling paint.

Soon afterward, Kingman Brewster made the announcement that has gone down in history as an index of the state of the universities and elite opinion of that era: "I am appalled and ashamed that things should have come to such a pass in this country that I am skeptical of the ability of black revolutionaries to achieve a fair trial anywhere in the United States." *Black revolutionaries.* In fact, they were terrorists and thugs. Or was Brewster expecting—in a sense, legitimizing—an armed insurrection against the American government? This was railing against the United States by a self-hating WASP. ("Railing" by WASP standards, of course.)

Panther leaders called for violence against the police. Weapons were stolen from National Guard trucks and a Connecticut sporting goods store, along with 140 pounds of fulminate of mercury (for blasting caps) from a Yale laboratory. Four thousand National Guardsmen were sent to Connecticut. Others, along with Marines and state troopers, made ready to help. The actual May Day event was an anticlimax—fifteen thousand demonstrators arrived, versus the half million who had been eagerly awaited. The demonstration was mainly peaceful, but the organizers made their point. New Haven had been made to look, for a few days, like a city in mid-insurrection.

Alex Rackley, by the way: his murder led to the trial of top Panthers that incensed Brewster and the rest. At the time, no one was terribly interested in Alex Rackley. Evidently he had been tied to a bed and questioned for two days under torture. Panthers had poured boiling water over him again and again, until finally he confessed to being an informer. Whereupon he was dragged out-side, shot in the head and dumped in a river.

But Rackley had never been an informer. It was all a mistake.

———

When did the painful split between the nation and its universities end? It never has. But if we move a generation forward and glance at the early 1990s, we find an academic world that has reached a bizarre stability. The doctrines of the cultural revolution have been internalized; academics carry them out without needing to think, or perhaps without being able to. These doctrines might have been reflexes originating deep in the neuromusculature, or rules learned by rote and executed without anyone's under-standing them. The cultural revolution made fools of America's universities and is still doing so.

In 1992, William Bennett (the former secretary of education) wrote that "the 'politically correct' mentality would be laugh-able if it weren't so serious and so pervasive," and he gave some examples:

> A proclamation banning "inappropriately directed laughter" and "conspicuous exclusion of students from conversations" was issued at the University of Connecticut.

> A controversy erupted at Harvard Law School when Ian MacNeil, a visiting professor, quoted Lord Byron: "And whispering, 'I ne'er will consent'—consented." The Harvard Women's Association was offended and denounced it as a "sexist insult."

And so on.[5] As Bennett notes, these things are different from the university outrages of the late 1960s. They are merely ludicrous, merely absurd, and smell slightly of plain insanity.

chapter seven

Today: Airheads and Obamacrats

If a man is articulate and intelligent, charming and successful and supremely self-confident . . . why would you ever suspect that he is also ignorant?—that he doesn't know what he's doing, doesn't know what he's talking about? How would you ever guess?

BARACK OBAMA AND HIS GENERATION OF AIRHEADS, THE FIRST EVER TO come of age after the cultural revolution, are unique in American history. All former leftist movements were driven by ideology. Obama's is driven by ignorance.

Conservatives like to think of Obamacrats as a short-term mistake they can attack and defeat; a house of straw they can huff and puff away. Conservatives won big, after all, in the midterm elections of 2010, and Obama himself might well lose when he's up for a second term in 2012. We're told that "the natural conservatism of America is already reasserting itself," which is like being told that "the natural dryness of the land is already reasserting itself" when you've scampered ten feet up the riverbank while the river is still rising, swelling, gorging itself, effortlessly lapping up dry land inch by inch. And when at last—much later—it disgorges the land it has consumed, everything will be different.

Obama is not important in himself, except insofar as he is black: the nation, both liberals and conservatives, took justifiable pride in having elected him. It was America's final exam in Tolerance School, and we aced it. But the man himself is merely a mouth for garden-variety left-liberal ideas—a mouth of distinction, a mouth in a million, but a mere mouth just the same. He is important not as statesman but as symptom, a dreadful warning. He is important not because he is exceptional but because he is typical. He *is* the new establishment; he represents the post–cultural revolution PORGI elite.

We have had left-wing presidents before. We've had failed presidents before; Jimmy Carter is a perfect example. Bill Clinton began his presidency as a left-liberal. The Obama presidency is different. Something has changed. Obama himself will go away like a bad cold, but there are many more where he comes from. Nowadays, a new generation of Obamacrats enters America's bloodstream every year, in late spring, when fresh college graduates scatter like eager little birds or puffs of dandelion seed to deliver a new crop of Airhead left-wingery to the nation and the world.

"The quality and content of the education provided is a clear indication of the quality and tendency of the democracy that provides it," wrote Lionel Trilling in 1952. A famous report called "A Nation at Risk," in 1983, put the nation on notice that its schools were failing. In 1987, Alan Bloom's widely read *The Closing of the American Mind* told Americans that their elite colleges were grossly politicized. The facts of educational decay were intolerable and all around us, like a mountainous garbage dump across the street on a hot day, with thousands of cawing crows spiraling cynically overhead and the stench of rot invading every last cubic inch. It took a powerful act of will to ignore the state of our schools, but we summoned up the will and we did it. And are still doing it.

Those famous reports of the 1980s, and others like them, described changes that had already happened. The big change in U.S. education happened mainly during the 1970s; it was widely and reliably reported in the 1980s—and has been largely ignored ever since. For roughly thirty years we have been aware of massive, portentous changes in how we educate our youth—and we have shrugged them off. And things have only got worse. American students learn little or no history or literature or civics. "Only a third of Americans can name the three branches of government," noted the former Supreme Court justice Sandra Day O'Connor. "But 75 percent of kids can tell you *American Idol* judges." We wince and move on.

"Education" is a boring topic; it's shiny vinyl floors and crash-slamming lockers full of vapid textbooks. Most conservative politicians and thinkers have concentrated on more exciting issues: the economy, federal and state government, the courts, foreign affairs. We know that our schools are failing; that we have failed our children, year after year after year. But how often do we think about the consequences?

Everyone agrees that President Obama is not only a man but a symbol. He is a symbol of America's decisive victory over bigotry. But he is also a symbol, a living embodiment, of the failure of American education and its ongoing replacement by political indoctrination. He is a symbol of the new American elite, the new establishment, where left-liberal politics is no longer a conviction, no longer a way of thinking: it is built-in mind-furniture you take for granted without needing to think.

How could thirty-plus years of educational malpractice *not* matter? It has already dyed the country a subtle shade of left, and the color will deepen every year.

The nation is filling inexorably with Airheads, nominally educated yet ignorant; trained and groomed like prize puppies to be good liberals. Old-time conviction liberals are being supplanted (as they age and die) by puppy-liberal Airheads. Old-time conviction conservatives are also being supplanted—by puppy-liberal Airheads. Politicized schools are one-way streets: they all go left. American schools are a bizarre echo of the old Soviet schools, which used to teach that, whatever the issue, the USA was always wrong. Now American schools teach that, whatever the issue, the USA is always wrong.

The collapse of American schools dates to the late 1960s and the 1970s. Students educated mainly or wholly under the new dispensation are now taking on senior roles in every part of American society. But the expanding legion of American Airheads don't know the sheer minimum a citizen must know in order to vote responsibly or serve in the U.S. government, let alone be president. Becoming a qualified American citizen with a minimal working knowledge of the nation's past is (apparently) not as easy as getting into Columbia or Harvard. The evidence is painfully clear.

A leading member of the Airhead contingent has spoken of "the bomb that fell on Pearl Harbor," as if the massive attack that nearly demolished America's Pacific Fleet consisted of *one* bomb. Maybe he was confusing Pearl Harbor with Hiroshima. (Sounds ridiculous, but modern teachers and academics tend to think of Pearl Harbor and Hiroshima as two examples of the same thing, gross aggression—Hiroshima being the worse by far.)

This same man once reported that his great-uncle had participated in the U.S. Army's liberation of the Auschwitz death camp. Auschwitz is in Poland. If the U.S. Army had indeed marched through Germany and all the way to Poland, if Americans instead of Russians had liberated Eastern Europe, the last half of the twentieth century would have been incalculably different. The Cold War would have taken a dramatically different shape.

What kind of mishmash inhabits this man's brain? He is (of course) Barack Obama. He describes himself as "a student of history."

Conservatives believe that today's liberals are ideologues. They have not grasped the colossal, terrifying truth. The words and actions of President Obama, and of many in his administration, don't even rise to the level of "ideological." Older liberals are ideologues, but modern Airhead liberals from Obama on down base their worldview, their political shtick, and all their intellectual bookings on ignorance. Their attitudes are learned by rote. Old-time elites used to choose the comfy furniture of liberal ideas to fit out their minds, but today's elites don't have to bother. Their minds—as they discover to their smug wonderment when they are old enough to look around—are prefurnished with built-ins! Of course, built-ins are much harder to get rid of than ordinary ideas; but who wants to get rid of them?

George Orwell saw the Spanish Civil War firsthand from the front lines, where he was fighting the Franco fascists. When he got back to England he said, "I saw newspapers in London retailing these lies"—false versions of the war in Spain—"and eager intellectuals building emotional superstructures over events that had never happened."[1] Events that *ought* to have happened, that *must* have happened, because left-wing theory said so. Hannah Arendt points out that political lies have a seductive selling point: having been concocted deliberately, they can easily be far more plausible than mere truth.[2]

Elsewhere, Orwell wrote, "My wife and I saw innocent people being thrown in prison merely because they were suspected of unorthodoxy. Yet on our return [from Spain] to England we found numerous sensible and well-informed observers believing the most fantastic accounts of conspiracy, treachery and sabotage which the press reported."[3] These friends of the Orwells, these "sensible and well-informed observers," were (naturally) intellectuals. Or as Lionel Trilling put it, "Those members of the intellectual class who prided themselves upon their political commitment were committed not to the fact but to the abstraction."[4]

Ari Goldman, formerly a reporter for the *New York Times* and now a journalism professor at Columbia, has revealed how a commitment to abstraction works in the American press. In 2011 he published a remarkable story exposing the truth about actions the *Times* had taken twenty years earlier.

Jews and blacks live in Crown Heights, Brooklyn; the Jews are mainly Chabad (or Lubavitcher) Hasidim. In 1991, when the neighborhood was about the same, a black child in Crown Heights was hit by a car and killed. The driver was a Chabad Jew. Like most such cases, it was a tragic accident. Some witnesses accused the driver of carelessness. Others denied that he had been careless. In any case, the incident was followed by what A. M. Rosenthal—the eminent former editor of the *Times* who had become a columnist—called a "pogrom." In a murderous three-day rampage by blacks in Crown Heights, a rabbinical student from Australia was knifed repeatedly and then beaten until his skull fractured; he died the same night. Many other Jews were injured, some seriously.

Despite what reporters on the scene wrote and said, the *Times* systematically lied about this murderous anti-Semitic riot—with the best intentions, naturally. The *Times* claimed that dangerous street violence had sprung up between Jews and blacks in Crown Heights. "Hasidim and blacks clashed in the Crown Heights section of Brooklyn through the day and into the night yesterday," read the opening sentence of a *Times* story about the riot. But this was "simply untrue," noted Goldman. "In all my reporting during the riots," he wrote in 2011, "I never saw—or heard of—any violence by Jews against blacks."[5]

The PORGI establishment had a theory: in the event of violence between blacks and whites, the whites are *at least* equally guilty. Case closed. The *New York Times* chose this theory instead of reality. It consistently referred to murderous anti-Jewish violence as a "clash" between whites and blacks, as if opposing mobs had met and battled; as if black gangs had *not* set upon unarmed Jews.

Just the same sort of lie was repeated in London, summer 2011. A black gang member was shot by the police, and several days of street violence followed. Evidently it was partly (not entirely) a race riot—gang violence committed by blacks. But the mainstream press retouched the truth to shield the public from reality and forbidden thoughts. The eminent historian David Starkey went on TV "and committed what *The Guardian* has called in a live blog 'career suicide,'" according to John Atherton on the ViewsHound blog. Starkey suggested that race might have been a factor in the riots.

What has changed between 1991 in Brooklyn and 2011 in London? *Nothing.* When intellectuals call the shots, when PORGIs are the establishment, newspapers will print lies rather than admit that their cherished, childish theories about the world are false. Yes, it's hard to admit you were wrong; it's hard to admit you've been childishly deluded. It's hard in all sorts of ways to be an adult.

Like many communities in recent years, Yale faithfully reports any crimes against its members. Every street crime is reported by mass email. Each account includes all the particulars, so students will know what to look out for—except that the race of the perpetrator is deliberately suppressed. And so everyone assumes, every time, that the criminals are black. The large majority of local criminals are indeed black. This game of we-all-know-but-can't-say sounds like harmless fun, but it leads to the kind of automatic self-censorship among younger people that's characteristic of police states. A black student published a piece in the school newspaper accusing *himself* of antiblack prejudice insofar as he was on his guard when a group of unknown black males approached on a dark street, but not when it was a group of unknown white males. Of course, that only means he is a rational human being. He'd be a fool to act differently.

Ian McEwan's novel *Saturday* (2005) centers on a middle-aged brain surgeon who drives past a street demonstration in London. The demonstrators are protesting Britain's and America's contemplated war on Saddam Hussein. "He might have been with [the demonstrators]," says the narrator, "if Professor Taleb hadn't needed an aneurysm clipped." This English surgeon had chanced to meet an exiled Iraqi professor who set him straight about Saddam's Iraq. Then he did some reading and discovered the "details of genocide in the north and south of the country, the ethnic cleansing, the vast system of informers, the bizarre tortures. . . . He concluded that viciousness had rarely been more inventive or systematic or widespread. Saddam's organizing principle was terror."

Without an exile to guide him, the man would have known nothing except lies. Yet the facts were on record all around him. They were everywhere. The establishment press had merely screened them out. The press had fed retouched truth to the public, in the spirit of Dr. Bowdler's Shakespeare. Bowdler expurgated Shakespeare to spare children the racy details. The establishment press expurgates the news to protect you from the truth. Thank goodness *they* can handle it!

Let's return to the early years of the Obama presidency. It's impossible for a president not to learn much on the job: highly concentrated, super-refined information is poured down his throat every day, gallon after gallon. But the things he said and did when he was newish to the job or still campaigning reveal the man himself, and tell us something about his passionate admirers.

Conservatives knew from extensive reporting—by newspapers, magazines, cable news, blogs—that Guantanamo was a well-run, humane, secure prison camp that made a special effort to accommodate Muslim inmates. "A total of twelve separate investigations over fifteen months have left no lingering doubt," wrote Arthur

Herman in 2009: "Gitmo is safer and less abusive than any deten-tion facility anywhere in the United States, military or civilian."[6] Those were the plain facts, meticulously documented. With the campaign behind him, what pressing reasons led the president to set these facts aside and announce that he would close the camp anyway?

Obama explained nothing; he merely proclaimed and decreed. In early 2009, he sent his attorney general to inspect Guantanamo yet again, after announcing it would be closed by a date certain. To evident surprise and confusion, the attorney general reported that Guantanamo was a well-run, humane, secure prison camp that made a special effort to accommodate Muslim inmates. The creeping suspicion began to grow, like the gathering shudder in a well-made horror film, that Obama had *actually believed* what he'd said during the campaign. He had actually believed that Guanta-namo was some sort of cruel, stinking hellhole.

What now? Obama, like so many others, had known only that (a) the world didn't like Guantanamo, and (b) America was nearly always wrong. Theoretically, Guantanamo was an awful camp and must be closed. Unfortunately (or not), the theory was wrong. But the theory was all he had. The president decreed policy based on wrong theories and ignorance.

In July 2009, a black Harvard professor was arrested by the Cambridge police when a neighbor mistook him for a house-breaker. The president said, "I don't know—not having been there and not seeing all the facts, but I think it's fair to say . . . that the Cambridge police acted stupidly." Actually, this was not fair to say. Obama didn't know what he was talking about. Just a minor shooting off of the presidential mouth? All presidents do it occa-sionally, but as for Obama . . .

In December 2009, when a terrorist was arrested in Detroit after trying to set off a bomb on an airplane, the president called him "an isolated extremist." Obama had already been told that Umar Farouk Abdulmutallab was connected to al-Qaeda in Yemen. Obviously he was not *isolated*. And he was no mere *extremist*. He was a terrorist and aspiring mass murderer. When the president made that "isolated extremist" comment, he didn't know what he was talking about. When the theories he has learned ("isolated extremists") clash with the facts (organized terrorism), he goes with the theories. And that's only natural. Education molds the mind and makes the man, and nothing hits us as hard ever again as the things we learn when we are young.

There is a pattern here. This president is not an ideologue; he does not reach that level. He is a PORGI Airhead: smart, educated, *ignorant*. And there is a deeper, underlying pattern. Obama has learned theories about the police versus black men. They are wrong. He has learned theories about the "real causes" of terrorism and about "isolated extremists" and "Islamophobia." They are wrong. He applied his theories just the way he was taught. But the theories, being wrong, gave him wrong answers. That is the PORGI elite, the new establishment.

In late 2009, Obama's attorney general decreed that the terrorist mastermind Khalid Sheikh Mohammed, Guantanamo's superstar mass murderer, should be tried not by military commission but in federal court, two blocks from the former World Trade Center. Both the attorney general and Obama were surprised when this proclamation was met by anger and disbelief, even among some Manhattan liberals. All good liberals know that the military is bad and the federal courts are good. The reasoning behind the announcement didn't seem to go any deeper than that.

Fact number one about terrorists is that they crave attention; they live for it and are willing (eager, delirious!) to kill for it and even die for it. We all want attention, but terrorism is the mad lust for attention transformed into pure evil. That's why terrorism exists: to make heroes, to rally support, to create celebrity. What lovelier gift for a terrorist mass murderer than a public trial in the media capital of the universe, instead of a brisk, orderly military hearing on some godforsaken Caribbean island? A public trial in downtown Manhattan would be as good as the slaughter of ten thousand innocents; even better! Allah be praised! But alas, alas. After more than a year of sulking and steaming, the attorney general reconsidered and reversed himself.

Of course, the decision had never been *considered* in the first place. Had there been reasons behind it, the administration would have laid them out, explained itself, won over at least some of its critics—whereas the number of its critics just kept growing. But there were no reasons behind the decree, only theory and dogma: Military bad, federal courts good.

In May 2011, the president made a speech in which he mentioned in passing that, in the natural course of things, Israel would return to her "1967 borders," with swaps here and there for fine-tuning. Then he seemed surprised—like the innocent he is, ensconced far above the battle on Mount Obama, watching the tiny ant-people tumble and play down below—when the Israelis exploded in furious incredulity. ("Lord," the president must have thought, "what fools these mortals be!")

Did the president even *know* that those 1967 borders were widely acknowledged to be indefensible? Did he know how they came about, in desperate fighting by the stupendously outnumbered, out-armed and out-trained Jewish community in Palestine, set upon by seven Arab armies the moment the state was declared, given up for lost by nearly everyone in the world who was paying attention? And how would Obama himself have gone about defending a nation whose waist was nine miles wide, beset with heavily armed enemies who reveled openly in the prospect of murder, mayhem and genocide? The skeletal Israel of 1948–1967, with its ribs sticking out and half its beloved capital sunk in enemy hands, where its synagogues were systematically destroyed and its graves desecrated—what did the president make of all that?

Or had he ever thought about it? Did he even know about it? But after all, these are mere facts, and facts are dog biscuits at the table of world-class intellectuals and the new establishment. Such persons have more important things than dog biscuits on their posh plates!

In summer 2011, the president spoke at a meeting of farmers in Atkinson, Illinois, and accepted questions from the audience. One farmer noted the ever-increasing burden of "rules and regulations" decreed by the administration, and said he feared worse to come. The president admonished him in the patronizing, omniscient tone that children find so infuriating when their parents and teachers spring it on them. "If you hear something is happening," said the president, "but it hasn't happened, don't always believe what you hear." Whereupon the audience burst into courteous laughter.

As of that summer, the EPA was writing new ozone regulations that would cost the country $19 billion per year by the EPA's own estimate, and other new rules dealing with boilers that would cost another $14 billion in upgraded equipment—and more were in preparation. The president then stepped in and squashed most of these lovely new rules. Will they stay squashed? It's anyone's guess. And the administration's big-gun regulation makers, its heavy artillery—the financial reform bill and Obamacare—had barely opened fire. So the president had been patronizing and arrogant to that audience of farmers, and he had also been wrong.

Obama has the gift of appointing people and making decisions in ways that spread airheadedness. NASA's antique fleet of space shuttles was breaking down, and at last the tow-trucks arrived to haul them off to the junkyards—or to museums, for exhibits on obsolescence and ancient history. George W. Bush had planned to revive NASA with a new moon mission, but Obama canceled it. Space exploration has never been his style. Three Apollo astronauts published an op-ed noting that the Obama administration was leaving NASA in "substantial disarray." As the last shuttle mission approached, with nothing on the schedule to follow— just a blank screen and elevator music while the audience shuffles out of the theater and one of the greatest projects in human history is unplugged and left for dead—the *Washington Post* quoted Bob Crippen, pilot of the first shuttle mission in 1981: "I've never seen NASA so screwed up as it is right now. . . . They don't know where they're going."[7]

With an Airhead president, the condition is catching.

——•——

Our news cycle erases the blackboard and starts over every fifteen seconds. But we need to remember what this president has said and done, the big things and the little ones. The little ones are sometimes the most revealing. In spring 2009, the president visited the queen of England and gave her an iPod preloaded with audio tracks including his speech at the 2004 Democratic National Convention and his 2009 inaugural address. (Perhaps by now the queen knows them by heart.) A month earlier Obama had dismissed from the Oval Office, in one of his first acts as president, a bust of Winston Churchill, on loan from Britain since 9/11. Churchill is said to have given some pretty good speeches too, but that was long ago. Taken together, the two actions made beautiful Airhead music, the two-part close harmony of vanity and ignorance.

During the 2008 campaign, Obama explained to "Joe the Plumber" that American tax policy should "spread the wealth around." From each according to his ability, to each according to his needs—the socialist creed. Redistributionist economic policies in, for example, Britain and Israel during the post–World War II generation had worked beautifully to brake those economies to a screeching stop, in acrid clouds of tire smoke. Maybe the president knows this, but maybe he doesn't. What's more important is the classic American line of thinking: I want to make good by my own efforts, not by virtue of some government leader doling out money that doesn't belong to him anyway. In Mary McCarthy's "Man in the Brooks Brothers Shirt," the wealthy businessman puts it simply: "Every workingman wants to live the way I do. He doesn't want me to live the way he does. You people go at it from the wrong end." He is dismissing 1930s-style socialism, but might just as well be dismissing Obama.

"I have a great horror of that kind of invidious jealousy which is at the bottom of the idea of redistribution," says the impoverished socialist hero of Henry James's *Princess Casamassima*. Here, James writes about "the ulcer of envy—the passion of a party which hung together for the purpose of despoiling another to its advantage." This has always been the spirit of the European redistributionist left. America has never seen things this way, but left-wing politicians keep hoping.

Did Obama actually believe in "spreading the wealth around," with all its moral and economic implications? Or had he never thought much about it one way or the other?

The story surrounding Obama's first nomination to the Supreme Court in May 2009 deserves telling. Sonia Sotomayor was a judge who believed herself to be specially qualified for the bench because she was Hispanic, female, and used to be poor. "I would hope," she had said, "that a wise Latina woman with the richness of her experiences would more often than not reach a better conclusion [on the bench] than a white male who hasn't lived that life."

(True, nearly all of us white males *do* spend our lives propped up in bed playing with our Xboxes and not having experiences—although some of us are said to have fallen, in the recent economic crisis, all the way down into the upper middle class and been expelled from our golf clubs and had our BMWs taken away; but let's hope that's only a rumor.)

Granted that the lives of wise Latina women are incomparably richer than those of mere white males, still: once Sotomayor has intuited, by dint of sheer racial brilliance and depth of experience, which party to a lawsuit is more *simpatico* and deserving, what then? Invite him to lunch? Friend him on Facebook? Treat him as innocent until proven guilty? There is a theory that "minorities" make better, wiser judges than other people. The theory is nonsense; the whole point of American justice is to judge people not

on *who they are* but on *what they did,* or didn't. A judge's oath stip-
ulates that "I will administer justice without respect to persons,
and do equal right to the poor and to the rich"; that "I will faithfully and impartially" do my duty. Impartiality is what justice has
meant to Western man since the Bible. "Thou shalt not respect
the person of the poor, nor honor the person of the mighty; thou
shalt judge thy neighbor *rightly*." (Leviticus 19:15.)

What higher cause compelled the president to set Western
civilization's concept of justice aside? Why was he so proud, so
inspired by a nominee who (so it seemed) could not possibly take
her oath of office seriously? He never answered these questions.
Apparently the meaning of justice has never occurred to him. (He
has more important things on his mind, dammit! *Why is he losing
Hispanic support?* There is an *important* question.) Obama is no
ideologue; he doesn't rise to that level. He merely applies the theories he has dutifully learned.

He believes that manmade climate change is a fact, and he
reared crushing new tax proposals on this rock-solid belief, obliv-
ious to the gathering scientific doubts that have forced ecofunda-
mentalists to stop talking about "global warming" and switch to
"climate change." (Meaning what?) When Democrats in Congress
said no to the huge energy tax called "Cap and Trade," it was time
for a pack of Obamacrat regulators to go yipping and yapping
after the sinners, and punish them by regulation.

It isn't that Obama has set aside those scientific doubts about
manmade climate change. More likely he has never heard of
them—making him just like the average high school senior or
college professor or network news anchorman; just as he hadn't
known what Guantanamo was like. It is a depth of ignorance that
is hard to grasp. How could *the president of the United States* be
ignorant of commonplace truths that every reader of objective,
unbiased news has known for years? Simple: the man is a PORGI
Airhead, the acclaimed leader of an Airhead generation.

Obama's ignorance is especially hard to see because he is
willing to speak falsehoods when he *does* know the truth. In a

week of bad economic news in spring 2011, he went to Ohio and made a speech about the federal rescue of the U.S. auto industry. The next day, the *Washington Post* ran this headline over a columnist's essay: "President Obama's phony accounting on the auto industry bailout." Sometimes he makes false claims on purpose. But don't let that obscure the fact that often he makes them in complete innocence. He actually thinks they are true.

———

It's hard to believe—it seems impossible—but the man we have elected president of the United States doesn't know what he's doing. Of course he is smart, dignified, can be articulate, can be charming, can be funny. When we see these attributes, moreover in *a president of the United States,* we take it for granted that he knows what he's about. When you are president, *obviously* you know the history of the United States and the modern world, and especially the long, sad series of events—from the First World War through the Second, and then the Cold War, and the strange, dangerous decades since—that created the political landscape we happen to live in. That, at a minimum, is what a president needs to know.

There's nothing unusual about these requirements. They are merely routine. That's why we take it for granted that any potential president just *knows* them. (Obama majored in political science.) And that, in turn, is why it is so difficult to grasp the truth about Obama. But he has so often spoken and acted as if he doesn't know what he is doing, hasn't mastered the minimum job requirements, that at last we have to face the truth. The man doesn't know enough to be president.

And after three years in office, the president is still at sea without his teleprompter. Back in May 2009, Vice President Biden lost his, and memorably ad-libbed, "What am I gonna tell the president when I tell him his teleprompter is broken? What will he do then?" Yet we all know that Obama is smart, articulate, coolheaded, a champion "communicator." How could such a man be hopeless at public speaking without a machine to lead him, word by word? Isn't speaking in public without a teleprompter exactly what smart, coolheaded, articulate men *do*? Obama needs his machine because he is an Airhead. He is smart, educated, *ignorant*.

This conclusion points to another, even more alarming. Obama graduated from some of the best schools in America: Columbia and Harvard Law. He isn't *especially* ignorant. He is only the leading citizen of an ignorant generation. What does that say about our schools? About America in general?

It says that we've had a cultural revolution. It happened long ago, but the consequences are still unfolding. In fact, this apple tree of a revolution is just beginning to bear rich ripe fruit, long after the showy blossoms have blown away.

chapter eight

Asymmetry and Balance

MANY OF US HAVE ALREADY FORGOTTEN THE EXPOSURE OF THE "JOURNO-list" group in summer 2010. Journolist was a listserv (a list of people broadcasting email within the group) made up of hundreds of reporters and academics. The members were mainly self-described liberals, some working for left-fringe news organizations, some for the mainstream. Here's one exchange, with names omitted. X, Y and Z are all prominent journalists.

> X: As a side note, does anyone know what prompted Michael Barone to go insane?
> Y: LEDEEN.
> Z: Let's just throw Ledeen against a wall. Or, *pace* Dr. Alterman, throw him through a plate glass window. I'll bet a little spot of violence would shut him right the f*** up, as with most bullies.

Z, who writes for the *Washington Independent,* had another inspired suggestion to help make the public forget the incendiary friendship between Obama and Jeremiah ("God damn America") Wright: pick some conservative at random, "Fred Barnes, Karl Rove, who cares—and call them racists." V, who works for National Public (*public!*) Radio, noted delicately that if she ever happened (God forbid) to see Rush Limbaugh collapse with a heart attack, she would "laugh loudly like a maniac and watch his eyes bug out." Thanks for sharing that, Ms. V. *That corpse you planted last year in your garden, / Has it begun to sprout?*

These are people who routinely call conservative or populist groups like the Tea Party "extremist." In fact, they do better than that: W, of the Bloomberg news agency, wrote: "Is anyone starting to see parallels here between the teabaggers and their tactics and the rise of the Brownshirts? Esp. now that it's getting violent? Reminds me of the Beer Hall fracases of the 1920s." So Tea Party people are not mere extremists, they're nascent Nazis—a comparison that is heavily sweat-stained with the ugliest kind of ignorance: ignorance not only of the Tea Party but of the Nazi party.

The ominous smell of hatred hangs in the air above left-wing journalism, like sour beer in a downscale Munich beer hall (if we must talk about Munich beer halls); like smoke from burning tires. A blaze of hatred lights up the modern left. This tire-fire has burned for a long time, but no one should be surprised. When you are programmed rather than inspired, when you have dogma instead of ideas, theories instead of facts, you need something to keep you going. Hatred is powerful fuel.

———

Many of us have forgotten that Dan Rather, brought down by his attacks on President Bush that were based on transparent forgeries and lies, saw the *Wall Street Journal* as right-wing and the *New York Times,* the Western world's leading left-wing paper, as mainstream. "An important thing to remember about the press," the former *Newsweek* editor Jon Meacham once told us, "is there is no ideological bias."[1]

But in 2008, we saw the mainstream media savaging John McCain and Sarah Palin, while showing unctuous reverence for Barack Obama. "The sheer bias in the print and television coverage of this election campaign is not just bewildering, but appalling," wrote Michael Malone, a commentator for ABC-TV's website. "And over the last few months I've found myself slowly moving from shaking my head at the obvious one-sided reporting, to actually shouting at the screen of my television and my laptop computer." Biased reporting of the historic '08 presidential campaign is a story in itself, including the media's indifference to the anti-American hate speech of Jeremiah Wright, and to the nature and meaning of Obama's relations with Bill Ayers, the unrepentant terrorist. During the campaign, the *New York Times* published an op-ed by Barack Obama, but refused to print one that John McCain submitted in response. (At Yale, each undergraduate gets a free copy of the *Times* every weekday morning.)

Sarah Palin hysteria was especially revealing, as accusations and smears by feminist bloggers descended past ugly to filthy and obscene. And it didn't stop after the election. In June 2011, the government of Alaska released more than ten thousand official emails to and from Governor Palin. Reporters converged from all over like wasps headed for a ten-ton chocolate sundae. The left-wingers among them—nearly everyone—must have arrived in Juneau faint with excitement. It was just like the Gold Rush of 1849, only this was a Stupidity Rush, a *Conservatives-Are-Imbeciles* Rush: the emails of Sarah Palin, Friend to the Clueless-and-IQless, Mrs. Moron herself! Vengeance for Journolist at last! Imagine the devastating disappointment, wrote Roby Harnden in Britain's *Telegraph,* when the mother lode revealed Palin to be "an idealistic, conscientious, humorous and humane woman slightly bemused by the world of politics. . . . If anything, Mrs. Palin seems likely to emerge from the scrutiny of the 24,000 pages, contained in six boxes and weighing 275 pounds, with her reputation considerably enhanced." The prominent Power Line blog wrote that the Palin emails had turned into "an embarrassment for legacy media."

Coverage of the Obama administration has been even worse than the campaign coverage. In June 2009, Phil Bronstein, a former editor of the (liberal) *San Francisco Chronicle,* posted a blog entry headed "Love or lust, Obama and the fawning press need to get a room." He remarked that "the Obama-press dance is a more consensual seduction where, in the old-fashioned sense, we're the girl." And he wondered, "Is there an actual limit to the number of instances you can be the cover of Newsweek?"

Also in 2009, Evan Thomas of *Newsweek,* reviewing the president's recent speech in Cairo, explained to MSNBC's Chris Matthews, "I mean in a way Obama's standing above the country, above—above the world, he's sort of God."

He's sort of God.

The tragedy of the atheist is that he is thrown back on his own resources to pick a god.

Peter Wehner commented that "it is now impossible to mock the media's adoration for Obama. . . . The depth and intensity of the passion for Obama among the press is something young children need to be shielded from."[2] After the Democrats were smashed in the midterm elections of November 2010; after the economic recovery had started to slip and slide and then roll backward in summer 2011 like a car attempting a slick hill that's too steep for it, Obama-worship was toned down just a bit in the mainstream press. But we'd best not forget what it was like—or what it revealed about the PORGI establishment.

Old-time left-wingers and right-wingers despised each other but recognized that they were comparable species, two points on a spectrum, with "the center" in between. They were old troopers who used to compete for the same Vaudeville bookings. But today's Airhead leftists know nothing of any political spectrum. They don't merely believe in the truth of their views and the falsehood of their opponents'. They classify themselves as rational and their opponents as irrational—buffoons like George Bush, Sarah Palin and Michele Bachmann, or thugs like Dick Cheney and Donald

Rumsfeld. The Airhead left, in their own view, are by definition the center, the responsible mainstream, the only sane place to be.

In August 2011, a television newsman on MSNBC interviewed a psychologist and "addiction expert" named Stanton Peele. Asked to evaluate Tea Party members, Peele said, "It reminds us of addiction because addicts are seeking something that they can't have." A little later he was asked, "So you're saying that they are delusional about the past and adamant about the future?" Stanton Peele replied, "They are adamant about achieving something that's unachievable, which reminds us of a couple of things. It reminds us of delusion and psychosis."

———

In modern America, asymmetry is the fundamental fact of political life. There is an Airhead left but no matching Airhead right. This is important, and hard to grasp because it's so odd: in modern America, *asymmetry is fundamental.* Obviously some conservatives are as stupid as some liberals; that's not the point. The point is that the left no longer tries to steer one way as the right steers the other. The left has jimmied the rudder so the ship of state is jammed on left, circling back toward the massive, drooling, dumb-dog government of the Jimmy Carter years.

Obama's health-care revolution was the biggest policy triumph of his first term. He wrote an eloquent commentary on this achievement when he announced the appointment, in summer 2010, of Professor Donald Berwick (Harvard) as head of the Centers for Medicare and Medicaid Services. Berwick had favored a single-payer system: *every* visit to *every* doctor by *every* American to be paid for by one single payer—the Feds. One payer, one ultimate decision maker, one father of the nation who writes all the checks and doles out everyone's allowance. One Superior Intelligence instead of the messy turmoil of economic freedom. (Berwick resigned at the end of 2011.)

No one has ever accused Obama and his Airheads of believing in democracy.

In fact, democracy-fatigue on the left is a growing part of the political landscape. The passage of Obamacare, in the teeth of repeated public attempts (in statewide elections) to say "stop," was a classic study in contempt of the public will. It was made complete by Speaker Pelosi's now-famous dictum that there would be plenty of time to read the bill once it had been passed (and you had nothing else to do as you whiled away the hours waiting endlessly for the services of federalized doctors).

There were other signs of the would-be intellectual elite's characteristic disdain for the public: the investing of Pontifex Maximus Sebelius at Health and Human Services with the power to set America's health-care course under Obamacare; the president's breezily encouraging Brazil to drill for oil off-shore while stifling America's own deep-water drilling and dismissing hard-pressed American drivers with *let them eat cake, or drive hybrids.* Commentators explain that the president is only playing to his left-wing base, as if that cleared him of responsibility; as if he hadn't chosen *them* every bit as much as they chose him.

In Wisconsin, the Democrats in the state senate literally walked out on democracy. Their gesture (and that of their Indiana colleagues) was eloquent; it said "To hell with democracy" more plainly than words ever could.

———

Obama is an Airhead and no ordinary ideologue, but he is certainly a left-liberal; he repeats the doctrine that he learned from left-liberal intellectuals. We speak of liberal and conservative as if they were mere political choices, but the difference goes deeper.

Deep down, to be liberal is female; girls want to be loved. To be conservative is male; boys want to be respected. (Does this proposition sound objectionable or outrageous? If so, that explains why no one says it, although it is perfectly obvious.)

Naturally we all have male and female attributes, and when I say that liberalism deep down is female, it goes without saying that deep female attributes can coexist with deep male ones. You can be roaringly, bearishly male and still liberal. But such people are more interesting than you might guess: each has a small hidden garden of femaleness tucked away somewhere deep inside his rough-hewn psyche. And you can be all woman and yet conservative, in which case you have a male sanctuary hidden away somewhere inside.

An ideology (left-wing, right-wing) is a set of beliefs that aren't rational like your belief in the basic laws of physics or biology, but aren't irrational either. An ideology is a projection of your personality; your ideology is *you* cast like a spotlight onto the cultural landscape in which you live. The scientific part of your worldview is an expression of facts, experience, evidence—at least second-hand; but an ideology is an expression of *you*.

Of course, girls like to be respected also, and boys to be loved. We are all human. But we order our needs and wants differently. Political urges have been taken up and expounded by philosophers, but their origins are psychological, not philosophical. Neither ideology is inherently superior. Liberals can do good and do evil; conservatives likewise.

Perhaps this sounds like a cynical rejection of all higher motives in politics. Not so. It is a simple fact that sometimes liberal policies (or those that are called "liberal" by consensus) have proven correct; sometimes conservative ones have. American liberals led the civil rights movement of the 1960s, and their belief in equal rights and an end to bigotry against blacks was right. Conservatives insisted that the Soviet Union was an evil empire, dangerous to mankind and to its own citizens; they believed that the Soviets could and must be defeated, not by war but by steadfastness. They were right, as were the anti-Soviet liberals, an important group in the 1950s who mostly died out afterward. It was a distinctly liberal president, Harry Truman, who committed the United States to the Cold War—and he had no inclination to press for civil rights.

President Lyndon Johnson was a liberal's liberal—but insisted that we fight the Communist invasion of South Vietnam. Richard Nixon was a conservative, but decreed an official policy of affirmative action.

It's obvious that anyone, man or woman, might be either a born liberal or a born conservative. On the other hand, Mary McCarthy's narrator in *The Group* (1963) reports that "most men she knew were Republicans," speaking of a Vassar '33 graduate; "it was almost part of being male." (McCarthy was a lifelong leftist, but her prose remains as fabulously alluring as her famous Vassar yearbook photo.) These "men she knew" were upper-crust males of the 1930s. Things change; yet in modern America, women have distinctly more liberal voting records than men do. Starting in 1964, relatively more women than men have voted for the Democrat in *every* presidential election. Since 1968, this "gender gap" has been larger than 5 percent each time except for 1976; in '92, '96 and 2000, the gap reached 10 percent or more. Your innate tendencies *can* be overridden by education or deliberate choice; you can be born right-handed and learn to be left-handed. Education counts heavily, but genes do too. At base, liberalism is genetic, and likewise conservatism. (Being either an intellectual or a thinker must have a large genetic component also.)

Liberal intellectuals tend to be insecure, to blame themselves, to curry favor. Like small girls, they are eager to feel loved, and worry lest they should not deserve it. They are eager to apologize and be forgiven. Naturally, liberal intellectuals invest the nation with these same desires. They apologize on behalf of America, blame America, want America to be loved.

Conservative intellectuals are proud, sometimes obnoxiously cocky, and don't like to apologize. They don't care about respectability; they want respect. "I have no doubt," the hero is told in Stendhal's *Charterhouse of Parma*, "that you will be a highly respected Bishop, if not a highly respectable one." Like small boys, conservatives don't want to be hugged and petted, and rarely crave affectionate forgiveness. They want to protect, not be protected.

Naturally, they invest the nation with these same desires. They want America to be respected.

No liberal foreign policy can succeed over the long term, because nations are not people, and no nation can be loved by other nations for very long. Its own citizens can love it as patriots, but that's different. Nations can, however, be respected over the long term.

A hunger for love versus respect is even more important to your view of domestic policy. Liberals want the government to love and care for each of its citizens; conservatives want the government to respect its citizens. Respect implies keeping your distance. In love there is no distance.

There is another way, more conventional but equally valuable, to understand the liberal versus conservative temperament. Some people's political instincts are dominated by outrage or sadness at what is wrong, or seems wrong, and others' are dominated by duty and devotion. "There does seem to be something in the liberal mind that is constantly at war with its circumstances and surroundings," writes Michael Walsh. "Now, one can (as liberals surely do) view this heroically, as a perpetual quest for justice in the teeth of an uncaring, unfeeling, unjust society. Or one can (as conservatives do) see perpetual rebellion as a form of arrested adolescence that combines imagined moral superiority with a peculiar kind of impotence."[3]

Or one can say that this "outrage instinct," whether or not it is adolescent, is good in itself but destructive in excess. All civilized people are outraged by injustice. Those who are especially outraged are indispensable. But liberal outrage can turn into left-liberal nihilism, meanness, hatred—and it has. ("Let's just throw Ledeen against a wall. Or, *pace* Dr. Alterman, throw him through a plate glass window." And this is sweet-talk compared to what's been said about George W. Bush, Dick Cheney or Sarah Palin.)

The duty and devotion of conservatives can also turn bad, and become complacency. Conservatives today are not complacent—but can't let themselves become complacent about complacency.

The Princess Casamassima is Henry James's luminously moving study of the delicate balance between liberal rage at injustice and conservative love of family, friends and country, of "the monuments and treasures of art . . . the conquests of learning and taste, the general fabric of civilization as we know it, based, if you will, upon all the despotisms, the cruelties, the exclusions, the monopolies and the rapacities of the past . . . ." Rage transforms itself into love in the novel, as hesitantly as a single green leaf changing color in the fall. Yet summer's green rage and fall's brilliant love are equally legitimate. Two passions, one man. Everyone is entitled to at least two.

Obviously America needs a left and a right. Any spectrum has two ends, and anyway there will always be people whose political instincts are dominated by outrage and others whose ideas are dominated by duty and devotion. The two parties have equal moral standing and equal importance to national life: we need the Prophets and the Psalms.

chapter nine

The Cultural Revolution Shapes America

MANY PEOPLE DON'T UNDERSTAND THAT THE CULTURAL REVOLUTION IS STILL an active force in American life. The first wave of revolutionary consequences wasn't over until the late 1980s. We are now seeing the second wave, as the Airhead generation—Obama and his followers—assumes power.

The president is an Airhead liberal who speaks out of ignorance and bases his opinions on nothing. His political views are unsound money, mere paper with nothing to back it. But unsound money is still money, and bad money can drive out good. And this is strange, because America, you would have thought, carted out left-liberalism with the trash long ago.

When Jimmy Carter's presidency ended in 1981, to a huge gasp of relief—a nationwide catharsis, as if the whole country had been riding on a defective airplane that was falling apart in midair but had somehow (miraculously) made it back to solid ground—left-liberalism seemed to be finished. Carter had passed through the American landscape like a drunken tornado and left the economy,

American power and American security smashed to hell. Not for many decades had the nation felt so low and so scared, as double-digit inflation forced people to worry every day about rising prices and the collapsing value of money, as unemployment approached 10 percent and mortgage interest rates approached 20 percent. As the Soviet empire surged, and the Islamic jihadists of Iran took and kept American hostages.

Then President Reagan took over—and when he departed in 1989, he left the nation in vastly better shape economically, militarily and spiritually. By the 1980s, conventional left-liberalism—with its big governments and high taxes, its foreign policy of chatting up your sworn enemies instead of defeating them—seemed like a rusty wreck up on concrete blocks, ready for the junkyard. Democrats discussed their need of a new worldview. "Neoliberalism" appeared. And then President Clinton took the stage in 1992 to demonstrate what a new-model Democrat looked like. After a bad start, in which he tried and failed to govern as a left-lib, he insisted that he was no old-time liberal, that "the era of big government is over," that he would govern from the center. He was a fairly popular president and a modestly successful one.

Soon after the second Iraq War began, the British prime minister Tony Blair obligingly arrived in Washington to complete this demonstration and explain what a liberal, post-left-wing foreign policy might be like. In July 2003, Blair told Congress:

> In some small corner of this vast country, in Nevada or Idaho, these places I've never been but always wanted to go, there's a guy getting on with his life, perfectly happily, minding his own business, saying to you the political leaders of this nation: why me? Why us? Why America? And the only answer is: because destiny put you in this place in history, in this moment in time and the task is yours to do.

The speech was taken as one of the most moving restatements in many years of the duties that accompany America's privileges as the richest, most powerful, most lavishly blessed nation in history.

So why should anyone choose to revisit the forlorn ruins of Jimmy Carter? Why should anyone set foot a second time on an airplane with a broken windshield, flat tires, and wings that are falling off, named *Leftward Ho!*? Yet a majority of the nation bought tickets and gamely climbed aboard. *Why?*

And why should states that had been conservative for decades suddenly turn, or trend, Democratic? Why should Virginia or North Carolina or Colorado move leftward? Of course, there were many abnormal ingredients in the 2008 election, the financial crisis above all. And 2012 will have its own kind of abnormality. But experts agree on the deeper, longer-term factors at work in these states. In areas like Virginia, young people are growing up or moving in who are more liberal and more likely to be Democrats than the older generation. Yet Virginia had been a conservative state for centuries; year after year, young people had voted more or less as their parents and elders had. What changed?

In 2008, Obama won 68 percent of the under-thirty vote, which is no mere victory, not even just a landslide (which usually means victory by fully 10 percent), not even a Senate-style "supermajority." This was a blowout, a complete Republican collapse. It was a foregone conclusion that Obama would win among young voters: he was youngish himself, charming and articulate, and youth is always for change. But the numbers are startling. Why did this happen?

Because the cultural revolution is bearing fruit and changing America.

During the revolution, American education—the colleges and graduate schools, the elementary schools and high schools—

changed fundamentally. America's schools used to be, for the most part, tentatively liberal. The revolution remade them.

So long as the educators are left-wing, the rest of the country could be 98 percent conservative and it wouldn't matter. The left-lib blot will spread; nothing can stop it. If the educators are left-wing, the nation must fill up inexorably with graduates who are left-wing, just like their teachers.

Obviously there are regional differences, class differences, household differences. But the best that centrists and conservatives can hope for, in the short and medium term, is a kind of armed truce, in which the country is split more or less down the middle. In this view, the cultural revolution carried the day over much of the East Coast and the West Coast and parts of the industrial Midwest—in Democratic states that were hospitable to the Big Change.

But cultural change is much deeper than politics, and more widespread. Civil rights is a done deal throughout the country— an extraordinary achievement. The cultural revolution didn't stop there, though. Attitudes toward sexuality and the family have changed, and modern feminism has carried its point nearly everywhere.

A woman has a right to enter any field for which she is qualified, and society has an interest in making sure she has that right. Males in particular have an interest, not just as citizens but as male citizens. Many (perhaps most) men prefer working with women; work better and more easily with women than with other men.

But a woman also has a right to devote herself to childrearing and homemaking, and society once again has an interest in making sure she has that right.

Feminism has created prejudice against women staying home—but that social pressure is small potatoes. The real prejudice against would-be full-time mothers comes not from society but from husbands. Give men a choice: more money because your wife works, or more loving care for your children because she doesn't? No contest. Most fathers love their children, but don't lose sleep over the details.

(In case this isn't obvious, consider: there are far more single mothers than single fathers in the world—why? Because most women don't have it in them to walk away from their own children. Large numbers of men do that all the time. Some unmarried women want a child so badly, they arrange to have one whatever it takes. How many unmarried men pine for a child?)

But the worst consequence of modern feminism for women themselves has been the cruel insistence that young men and women be treated as if they wanted the same things and saw life the same way. And which things should they want? How should they see life? They should want *male* things, of course (the *feministas* ordained), and see life the male way. Men want as much sex as they can get, period. Women usually want children and, therefore, a liaison with some man who will be a father for the duration of the child's career and not just the first twenty minutes. Society—men and women—used to back up women who said no: not until I can trust you over the long term. Feminists kicked out those props, and the whole social structure of courtship collapsed into bloody-minded chaos.

For men, it has been paradise.

In the 1930s, some younger leftists—especially Marxists—believed in "free unions." Instead of getting married, couples would live together as long as they liked, then separate without ceremony. Today the phrase is dead but the idea has triumphed. People still get married, of course, but young people feel free to live together and part when they choose—as they have for decades. *Free unions.* Run-of-the-mill liberals of the 1930s (as opposed to hard-leftists) would have been scandalized.

As Norman Podhoretz wrote in 1979, "if the Movement is dead, which in a formal sense it certainly is, it died as much because it won as because it lost. Its ideas and attitudes are now everywhere."[1]

On social and cultural and environmental issues, conservatives nearly everywhere have grown less conservative. The message of the cultural revolution is sinking in. Mary McCarthy: "A scandal could be counted on that would cause a liberal lady somewhere to strike the college from her will."[2] This is the 1952 novel *The Groves of Academe,* and the question is: what might a rich *liberal* lady find scandalous in 1952? Answer: "A pregnant girl . . . alleged racial discrimination, charges of alcoholism or homosexuality . . . ." In recent years, liberals and most conservatives have accepted the cultural revolution's idea that no stigma attaches to an unmarried woman's having a child. Bill Clinton's proposals to allow openly homosexual servicemen in the armed forces generated aggressive criticism in 1993, and the proposal was withdrawn; eighteen years later, Barack Obama's announcement of the same policy drew only low-key objections from most conservatives.

Having moved left, won its point and planted its flag, the new establishment naturally plans its next advance, aiming even further leftward. A generation ago, the idea of homosexual marriage wasn't even part of the hard left's agenda. (A generation ago, too, advocates of homosexual marriage would have needed better arguments than today's favorites; the public's tolerance for speciousness and non sequiturs increases as the schools collapse.) Today, most PORGIs take it for granted that homosexual marriage should be legal. To many people it seems just *obvious* that such a transformation would help some and hurt none, and so we are wrong to stand in the way.

Does equality mean that *everyone,* every adult, has the right to get married? Of course. And everyone already has that right. Does equality mean that everyone has the right to define marriage to suit himself? It never has before. Maybe our view of marriage should change—but could we discuss it first?

Here is a strange anomaly: PORGIs have learned that one must always be careful, cautious, conservative in making any change to the natural environment. Even the smallest change, innocent and seemingly benign, can have bad consequences in the long run. So how can PORGIs be so tone-deaf to the human ecosystem, also known as "society"? Why doesn't it occur to them that changes to this delicately balanced system must also never be reckless or blind?

Where is the social impact statement regarding homosexual marriage? Why should such projections be required for the natural but never the human environment? At a time when the idea of family is more rickety, less stable than it has been in hundreds, perhaps thousands of years, might a change in the definition of marriage gratify a smallish minority but bring grief in the long term to many more people over many generations? The idea of marriage is currency in American society, legal tender, like the dollar but incomparably more important. If we tamper with the definition, we affect every man, woman and child in the country. Adulterating the definition makes the thing itself less important. Why should a nation that has grown so monumentally cautious when it comes to meddling with nature meddle so recklessly with society?

One thing we know for sure: what seems ludicrous or impossible today will eventually be a dead-serious proposal *if* it lies on the great road leftward. In summer 2011, a meeting of American psychiatrists discussed lowering the heat under pederasty. *Mild* desires for sex with children would no longer be grounds for anyone's getting worked up. (How mild?) A group of psychiatrists recommending this change posted a statement on its website:

> Stigmatizing and stereotyping minor-attracted people inflames the fears of minor-attracted people, mental health professionals and the public, without contributing to an understanding of minor-attracted people or the issue of child sexual abuse.

Why get excited (say these people, who evidently have never heard of pronouns) merely because your fellow citizen has a *mild* preference—all things considered, just a tie-breaker when you can't quite make up your mind—for ten-year-olds? (*Lolita* will have to be rewritten.) Onlookers at recent meetings of the American Psychiatric Association report that decriminalizing pederasty is openly discussed. Recall that one of the first punches landed in the modern struggle over homosexuality was the APA's decision in 1973 to delete (with due ceremony) "homosexuality" from its list of psychological disorders. Occasionally crimes are decriminalized, but it's not often that an illness is depathologized. Thereafter, homosexuality was merely, by expert decree, another kind of normal.

Maybe that's good. The line between normal and abnormal is always, in some degree, arbitrary. I spend much of my time in the art world, where I hope to be as tolerant of my homosexual friends as they generally are of me. "Besides, Monsieur," the narrator is told in Proust's *In Search of Lost Time,* "the greatest folly of all is to mock or condemn in others what one does not happen to feel oneself."[3] The problem is merely the new establishment and its contempt for democracy.

Intellectuals don't believe that society should argue the whereabouts of the all-important line between normal and abnormal. They believe its location should be determined by the experts, imposed by the judges, proclaimed by the establishment and obediently accepted by the hicks—sorry, I meant by *the population at large.* The left would prefer America to become a Venetian Republic, where the establishment (or nobility) elects the president (or doge), who follows the establishment's instructions; and everyone else shuts his mouth. And keeps out of Tea Parties if he knows what's good for him. "President Obama, this is your army," said Teamsters president Jimmy Hoffa in fall 2011. "We are ready to march. Let's take these son-of-bitches out." *Banzai!*

Part of the left's new agenda is reparations to blacks for slavery. Rahm Emanuel, mayor of Chicago and former Obama chief of staff, has endorsed this idea of compensation payments to the descendants of former slaves. The theory holds, evidently, that nonperpetrators must compensate nonvictims for crimes they never suffered—but would have, if they had been born two hundred years ago. (Probably. But this is only a detail.) Perhaps someone owes *you* money for a crime he never committed, but would have, if only you had both been born in some other century. Think of the possibilities!

The left would love to strike "In God We Trust" from U.S. currency. (The phrase comes from the last verse of the *Star Spangled Banner,* which ought to be sung more often.) They would love to remove "under God" from the Pledge of Allegiance. (That phrase, of course, is Lincoln's.) There will be many more incidents like the one in June 2011, when NBC television cut "under God" from the rendition of the Pledge it used as a prelude to the U.S. Open golf tournament, and then apologized. The omission, said NBC, "was not done to upset anyone." (We are awfully sorry to have knifed your friend to death. It was not done to upset anyone.) In this way advanced scouts feel out enemy territory, then scurry back to their own lines until the army is ready to move.

The left also has ambitious ideas for new environmental regulation. "Animal rights" is a fertile field; so is "children's rights"; and many, many more. Should illegal aliens be allowed to vote? The mayor of New Haven thinks so. Should pineapples be allowed to marry?—or at the very least, no longer be derided as *prickly?* Inventing rights has become one of the intelligentsia's most promising growth fields. It is challenging and fun.

If Obama does not get his whole program accomplished, another even-lefter president will arise before long. The establishment is no longer WASP-conservative; it is PORGI-liberal. And that has made all the difference.

The vast group of Americans we might call the Airhead Army is hard to define precisely, which partly explains why so little attention has been paid to it. The army consists of Americans who were mostly born after 1960. Its oldest members are now reaching the age at which people traditionally become CEOs, senators, cabinet secretaries, college presidents, generals, admirals, all-around big-shots. The Airheads partly overlap the usual definition of "baby boomer"—boomers were born between 1945 and 1965; but Air-heads, young and old, share an experience far more important than anything the boomers share.

Is everyone under fifty (most of America) a left-liberal Airhead? Of course not. The postrevolutionary generation includes a large variety of people, the steadfastly apolitical and the stubbornly con-servative among them. But left-liberal Airheads are a huge pres-ence, and the establishment is theirs.

What do the Airheads share? What defines them?

All were educated *after* the cultural revolution had started to wind down—and ironically, started to be noticed—beginning around 1966. In that year, America's military presence in Vietnam reached half a million men, and antiwar demonstrations became regular, large-scale events. Race riots broke out in Atlanta, and the Black Panthers were organized. The Supreme Court imposed Miranda rights to protect suspects in criminal cases. The change in the nation's sexual mores accelerated. These were all conse-quences of America's cultural revolution. Meanwhile, in Com-munist China, Chairman Mao launched a brutal, bloody purge of teachers and intellectuals, which he called the Cultural Revolution.

During the 1970s, many left-wing teachers taught their political beliefs—the message of America's own cultural revolution—to their students. Those students were the leading edge of the Air-head Army. Among this leading edge, some graduated to become teachers themselves. They handed the message on to *their* stu-dents. Every year saw a new group of students emerge for whom the message of the revolution seemed less like radical left-wing politics and more like simple truth. *In modern America, the left gets its way not by convincing people but by indoctrinating their children.*

Back in the 1970s, radical schoolteachers and college professors knew they were radicals; knew they were perched at the left edge of the balance beam. Things would be different for their students, because by the 1990s the cultural revolution had already happened.

In summer 2006, at an academic meeting, Harvard's president Lawrence Summers wondered whether the far larger number of male than female scientists might not reflect some built-in property of most men versus most women. He didn't endorse the idea; he simply wondered. His comments, according to the *Boston Globe,* "sparked international outrage."[4] Accordingly Summers abased himself, apologized profusely and acknowledged that he had acted like a dangerous crackpot lunatic, betraying the revolution and disgracing the university and himself. But he was sentenced to the maximum anyway: he was forced to resign the presidency and was *sent away from Harvard,* for a full year. At that point, Summers (no doubt) only wished that his feminist opponents had demanded the death sentence.

Feminists are famous for their take-no-prisoners fury, which I have known firsthand; they are *the* deadliest enemies. A generation ago, Martin Amis wrote that "to challenge feminism, in America, in 1984, is to disqualify yourself as a moral contender. It is the equivalent of espousing a return to slavery."[5] There are fewer doctrinaire feminists now than in 1984, but the same total fury poured into fewer vessels yields an eye-opening increase in rage-per-feminist.

Where foundational left-wing doctrine is concerned—for example, that male and female are interchangeable—the message is simple. Wondering is forbidden. Got that? *Forbidden.* In the Age of Airheads now approaching, such embarrassing accidents as the Summers episode won't happen. Forbidden ideas simply *won't occur* to the Harvard presidents of tomorrow. They will have grown up free of error, free of sin, free to enjoy the future with open hearts and empty minds.

(The wondering ban instituted by modern academics leaves an obvious question. What kind of experimental result would convince a PORGI that his intuitions about male and female are wrong? That men and women are *not* interchangeable, not intellectually equivalent? Answer: no kind of experiment, because such assertions are true by decree, and will stay true unless and until the decree is rescinded. So if you were planning to look for evidence, don't bother. This sort of corrupt thinking spreads like cockroaches.)

Obama is the perfect model for a modern Harvard president. Had he lost the 2008 presidential race, Harvard would have been an obvious next job for him. *He* would never have been visited by wrong thoughts of the sort that undid poor Larry Summers. (From Obama's inauguration until late 2010, the sorry Summers was chairman of the National Economic Council. Some journalists guessed that he would have been Obama's treasury secretary, as he had previously been Bill Clinton's—if he hadn't lost his head and disgraced himself that ill-famed summer's day in '06.)

The philosopher Julian Young was brave enough to chance it (feeling his way carefully) with forbidden thoughts, and has survived so far. In his fine recent biography of Nietzsche he ventured, "It *might* really be true that men are better at some things and women at others" (emphasis in the original).[6] Hear the tone: Young tiptoes up to the truth as if it were packed with dynamite on a short fuse. Could such a thing as *men being better at some things and women at others* really be? We thought it was sheer fantasy; that's what our teachers told us!

Yet this radical idea, to be mooted in whispers behind closed doors, is a commonplace well known to every three-year-old. Every three-year-old has noticed that men have more raw aggression than women, and that high aggression is good for some things (like playing football) and bad for others (like caring for three-year-olds). For intellectuals, the bright light of theory blocks out mere common sense.

The intellectual's odd starting point—replace facts with theories—leads him to conclude that the relative shortage of female mathematicians, engineers, orchestra leaders and chess champions must reflect a relentless though fiendishly undetectable antifemale bigotry in universities, music schools and chess clubs. Like a physicist whose theories tell him that some particle *must* exist, establishment intellectuals know for sure that antifeminism has somehow got loose in the nation's music schools, even though no one can actually find it.

The moral problem here is Young's: those who agree with him clearly believe that male specialties are somehow better and worthier than female ones. Otherwise, why should colleges like Yale press girls to major in physics or engineering, and not press boys to major in English? And why is it Yale's business, anyway, what Yale girls (as opposed to Yale students) choose to major in? There is bigotry at work today in the hard sciences and technology: bigotry against young men. In practical terms, it probably doesn't matter much; it only affects the occasional student here and there. A life here, a life there—what does that matter when theory is calling the shots? But once upon a time we used to oppose bigotry on principle.

"Undetectable bigotry," the province of Voodoo Sociology, is crucial to the left-liberal worldview: the theoretical prediction that some type of bigotry *must* exist outweighs any amount of mere evidence that it doesn't. For establishment PORGIs, theoretical predictions are shiny brass scale-weights, hefty and solid and cool in your palm, while facts are the fluffiest sort of feather; empty a whole pillow's worth into the balance pan and they still don't outweigh one shiny brass prediction.

In 2006, three white members of the Duke University lacrosse team were indicted on charges of having raped a black dancer. The charges seemed fishy from the start, and were eventually thrown out. But in the meantime, Duke's president, Richard Brodhead, publicly took sides against the athletes. Many Duke professors and students denounced them as racist louts. Airheads all learn the doctrine that in any black-versus-white dispute, blacks are right—unless they are conservative, in which case they are not black. (Recall our child theoretician and his non-red not-a-rose.) Airheads also learn that in any man-versus-woman dispute, the woman is right. In theory, the Duke case was a slam-dunk.

Many saw Barack Obama versus John McCain as a black-versus-white dispute. Some also saw Obama versus Hillary Clinton in those terms. At a minimum, *it has helped Obama, politically, to be black*. Can't we all just grow up and admit it? Of course not. Speaking this simple, self-evident truth could practically get you assaulted in establishment circles (or, *pace* Dr. Alterman, thrown through a plate glass window).

Airheads have trouble telling fact from opinion, and common wisdom from partisan politics. When candidate Obama spoke of being "post-political" or "beyond politics," he might easily have meant: "My views are not political; they are just common sense, received wisdom, the simple truth. Only Republicans make political statements. I am a simple truth-teller."

Where theory guides you, facts don't count, don't matter, don't *exist*. That is the way intellectuals act, and they have imparted this worldview to the intellectual*izers,* the PORGI Airheads, who do the dirty work.

"The mediocre American is possessed by the present and the mediocre European by the past," Auden wrote.[7] History has never been an American specialty, but Airheads take American indifference to history a step further. They are ignorant of the past.

The implications for America are profound. Suppose you were suddenly struck by amnesia (which is usually a comedy routine; but suppose it happened). You know nothing about yourself beyond what you observe. Your memories and your past are gone. Without memories and a past, you are no one; your personality has been erased. King Lear's deliberately *dismissing* his past—his powers, his position, the people who are dearest to him—creates the crisis of absent personhood that occupies the center of the center of Western literature:

> Doth any here know me? This is not Lear.
> Doth Lear walk thus? speak thus? Where are his eyes?
> Either his notion weakens, his discernings
> Are lethargied—Ha! waking? 'Tis not so!
> *Who is it that can tell me who I am?*

(My italics.) With no past, you are no one. And a nation without a past is likewise stripped of identity. Failing to teach the nation's past means suppressing its identity. Failing to teach America's history makes America faceless, a mere generic Western nation, Xtra-Large; globalism becomes natural and patriotism impossible. Suppressing history means suppressing America and Americanism.

Learning history, literature and religion complicates the simple pieties of the cultural revolution. Airheads have accordingly done their best to eliminate these subjects. Teaching American history, aside from a few marvelously evil incidents out of context, is dangerous to a basic tenet of the cultural revolution and must accordingly be stopped. Nearly all cultural revolutionaries believe that America is at best nothing special, and often a wicked bully. PORGI Airheads found it hard to get excited about Obama's sitting still and listening quietly to a black preacher scream "God damn America!" Most had listened quietly themselves to the same sort of statements (perhaps less concisely expressed) plenty of times.

Every member of the Airhead Army has learned about America's shameful history of slavery and antiblack bigotry. It's right that they should. But a proper study of American history ruins the simple, childlike pieties of the cultural revolution. Students are not taught that America invented modern democracy; or they are taught not to care. They are not taught that Americans struggled and suffered and died by the hundreds of thousands to free the slaves. That America rescued England and France from defeat by Germany in the First World War, and did it again in the Second while simultaneously liberating Asia and the Pacific from unspeakably bloody and bestial Japanese rule. That America all but eradicated race prejudice in a single generation, and won the Cold War against the evil empire of Soviet Russia. Not such a bad record. It makes you think—though Airheads would rather do anything but that.

In *Notes on the State of Virginia* (1783), Thomas Jefferson explains that as soon as children have learned the basics of reading, writing and figuring, the first phase of their education should be "chiefly historical"; young minds are "to be stored with the most useful facts of Greek, Roman, European and American history." (*Thomas Jefferson* insisting that children must learn *facts* about history? The left reels. Was he drunk, or just kidding?) "History by apprising them of the past will enable them to judge the future," writes Jefferson; "it will avail them of the experiences of other times and nations; it will qualify them as judges of the actions and designs of men." It will teach them what an American is—in other words, who *they* are.

The peerless eighteenth-century author and thinker Samuel Johnson writes,

> the truth is that the knowledge of external nature, and the science which that knowledge requires or includes, are not the great or frequent business of the human mind. Whether we provide for action or conversation, whether we wish to be useful or pleasing, the first requisite is the religious and moral knowledge of right and wrong; the next is an acquaintance with the history of mankind. . . . Prudence and justice are virtues and excellences of all times and of all

places; we are perpetually moralists, but we are geo-
metricians only by chance.

If they know nothing else, Americans need to know ethics and
history. But these are the Airheads' weakest topics: religious and
moral knowledge of right and wrong; acquaintance with the history of mankind.

When Obama was asked at what point a baby gets "human rights,"
he declined to answer and described the question as "above my
pay grade." Many Airheads are post-Christians or post-atheists for
whom the existence or nonexistence of God is too unimportant
to think about. If you are torn out of history, unplanted and
uprooted, your natural loyalties to your nation and religious community disappear. You can float free and easy like a helium bal-
loon above ordinary people and their little loyalties. You can live
for the moment, flying high, having fun and drifting comfortably
with all the other helium balloons. PORGI Airheads have been
liberated from history, from their national and religious identi-
ties, from their religious communities.

Cut off from history and their own national and religious traditions, Airheads become "globalists" adrift on the amoral seas of
international business, where such ideas as liberty and truth, justice and democracy are either dead weight or liabilities. They can
be deal killers with nations like Communist China, Saudi Arabia
and others that cannot stomach the American ideals of liberty,
equality and democracy.

Among Airheads, patriotism is simply vulgar, like trailer
parks or Christianity. The goal of the National Council for Social
Studies, says Kay Hymowitz, is for American students to see
themselves as citizens of the world, not of America. A keynote
speaker at an NCSS conference "warned against patriotic displays

like the singing of 'God Bless America.' 'The Swedes,' he noted, 'and the Kenyans don't think God blesses America over all other countries.'"[8] Obviously this person doesn't quite understand English, but let that go. Love of America and its principles is off the educational agenda nowadays.

Will the post-moral, post-patriotic Airhead Army care for and protect this nation, when it has been reared to feel no more attachment to the United States than to a pet goldfish or a comfortable pair of socks?

PORGI Airheads see America as a mere multicultural grab bag with no more unity or purpose than the "gorgeous mosaic" inside a box of assorted cookies. And every other nation is assumed to be the same. An Airhead paradox: for all their love of "diversity," Airheads assume that everyone in the world is just like them. Hence their inability to grasp even the most basic facts about terrorism or jihadist Islam; hence their plans for sitting down with murderous dictators (of Syria, Iran, Venezuela, North Korea) for friendly chats. This was Neville Chamberlain's view of the world.

We have knowingly reared a whole generation in ignorance of history, literature, religion, morality. "They have sown the wind, and shall reap the whirlwind." (Hosea 8:7.)

The Airhead generation, together with its leader, has been inoculated with theories against facts. The Airhead generation was reared ignorant of the past, and therefore of themselves. The Airheads—polished and plausible and articulate, but terribly innocent, terribly ignorant—are taking over America.

Enfin, je demanderai pardon pour m'être nourri de mensonge. (Rimbaud.) "In the end, I will ask forgiveness for having been nourished on lies." An epitaph for Obama, and his whole generation.

Where Does That Leave Us?

WE ARE FACING A TERRIBLE PROBLEM WITH A FAIRLY SIMPLE SOLUTION. But the problem must be solved soon, or we lose a crucial advantage. There are still plenty of people around who were educated before the cultural revolution and remember the way we were: our schools, colleges, the press and the civilized world generally striving—with partial success at best, but fine persistence—to tell the truth. Principled conservatives *and* liberals remember it all fondly. They don't want to move backward in time. They don't want to restore an old world; they want to build a new one that we can be as proud of as William DeVane was proud of America in 1957. We want a country whose national leaders are known for "integrity, idealism and skill"; where American arts, sciences and technologies continue to lead the world; where our college teachers are "learned and devoted"; where America herself is "the wonder and envy of other nations."

In short: We want to go back to telling the truth.

As always, a fair number of young people are standing by, eager to help overturn the garbage truck of modern education just for the fun of it. Old and young against the center is a potent combination. One thinks of Henry James's *The Awkward Age,* in some ways his greatest novel, in which old and young quietly, resolutely combine against the corrupt middle.

Of course, conservatives are likely to be the driving force in the Truth Revolution. Far more conservatives than liberals are willing to quarrel with the long trajectory of modern culture. Since the train is headed in a leftward direction, liberals don't get worked up about where it's going.

But conservatives are themselves hindered from getting serious about basic cultural problems when the short-term ups and downs of politics are so absorbing. If you find yourself bobbing in a life-jacket in the middle of the North Atlantic in winter, you too will find it hard to worry about the long-term drift of the currents. In fact, you might find it hard to see over the next wave. Liberals have the same tendency. For now, they usually associate liberalism with Barack Obama and the Democratic Party, while conservatives focus on their chances of beating the Democrats and Obama in November 2012—and on their growing disdain for the man him-self, as he crumples under pressure like a Buick in a car-crusher. Obama grows testier and more patronizing all the time, and more self-absorbed—although on the day of his inauguration he was already, experts hypothesize, the most self-absorbed man since the Middle Bronze Age. "I would put our legislative and foreign policy accomplishments in our first two years against any president— with the possible exceptions of Johnson, F.D.R., and Lincoln," the president told an interviewer in December 2011, "—just in terms of what we've gotten done in modern history." Because he names Lincoln, it's obvious that "modern history" is intended not to limit the president's greatness but to emphasize that his feats were achieved on an especially difficult battlefield.

But none of this matters, much. What matters is that America is in trouble. To right the nation, conservatives need to follow a favorite liberal rule and *look for the root cause.* And here it is:

- With each passing year, the proportion of Americans who were educated *after* the cultural revolution increases; and such people are abnormally likely to be left-liberals—not by reasoned conviction but by indoctrination.

The solution to this deep problem is simple and urgent. Here is my one-point program for curing America.

1. American education is in the hands of liberal Airheads. Take it away from them.

In one way, it is the perfect time for such a transition, while much of American education is being transformed by the onslaught of the internet. True, it's far better to learn from a human being than from a machine: the character of the teacher is nearly always more important than the topic being taught. But a flawed solution is better than none. The internet will let parents guide their children's education, or at least choose a guide they trust. A new breed of education mentors will emerge: schools or churches, think tanks or professional organizations, or a new kind of entrepreneur. Anyone who can convince parents that he knows the vast and fast-expanding world of online classes and institutions, and has his own trustworthy philosophy of education, can set up as a mentor or guide. As we enter the first free market for education in history, such mentors will be important. Some will acquire the same sort of reputation that famous schools and professors have today.

Of course, the new net-centered education world will develop its own face-to-face gatherings. Not everything will happen by remote control. Some gatherings will be groups of students of different ages, each enrolled in a separate collection of online courses, but all from the same neighborhood. These new one-room neighborhood schools will be presided over by any responsible adult who can supervise a group of computer-learners. The students share lunchtime and recess and the Pledge of Allegiance, and not much else, except their small schoolroom close to home. Other gatherings will be now-and-then meetings of students whose educations do overlap: students who share the same mentor, for example.

For college students, "internet hostels" are bound to sprout in places that college students like: Manhattan or Paris, London or Rome or L.A., or anywhere near a beach. They provide room, board, hot spots and a modicum of adult supervision. They are likely to be controversial at the start, as "adequate supervision" is fought over—the surrounding towns wanting more, the hostel companies and the students fighting for less. In this respect, it will be a rerun of the Middle Ages in Paris or Oxford or Cambridge. And it will all be worked out. In the meantime, college students can learn online at home or anywhere they like.

But this all leaves a problem. The only schools that are guaranteed to survive this upheaval are elite universities. They sell a product that is almost worth the price: pure 24-karat prestige. But they were the prime movers of the cultural revolution in the first place, and are still the leaders. What good will it do to scrap *nearly* the whole works if the most dangerous bits survive?

The top universities will sail right through this gigantic internet gale and come out slightly roughed up and seasick, but stronger. The goal of many of these institutions today is to transform themselves into "global universities," and here is what that means: they want to become *not American*. And the internet will help them reach this goal.

Today, top universities are opening campuses all over the place, especially in rich Arab nations and up-and-coming Asian powers. The internet, when they learn to use it intelligently—which so far they haven't—is just the tool to help them smudge over the boundaries between home and away; to blend all the far-flung branches of Magnificent U. into one global institution. America, the platinum-card deans and presidents and trustees figure, is a played-out brand. *It's not 1957 anymore!* The universities themselves have seen to that. Glorious U. longs to pull free from the moorings of national identity, to become a freedom-aspiring, liberty-drunk dirigible bent on sailing the vast skies of the world at large, far *far* above such trivial details as national identity. It wants to be looked-up-to by everyone.

The deans and trustees are pathetically wrong about America. However much they denounce the USA, American life is what the peoples of the world yearn to lead. But America's elite universities (plus a few European ones) will nonetheless succeed in denationalizing themselves, and they will thrive.

The natural instinct of concerned conservatives is to attack the elite schools, to gnaw away at their maniacal leftness one twig at a time. It's a worthy project and can only do good. But here is my one-point strategy for *accomplishing* my one-point plan to fix America:

1. Focus on internet education!

True, the top schools will continue to wield a huge influence. But reborn grade schools will produce students who are not the ignorant, half-baked pushovers of today. And the ed schools will steadily weaken.

American internet education will come to reflect the generally conservative nation. The neutral or mildly right-leaning internet grade schools and colleges will tug against the unreconstructed reactionary left of the elite universities. Today the fix is in; tomorrow, in the internet future, conservative ideas will have a fighting chance—*if* the conservative intelligentsia and leadership manage to get interested in education and American culture.

As WASPs become a minority in this nation they made, we will need to study and understand them; we will no longer be able to take them for granted. For one thing, we will need to understand that self-hating WASPs are as important a phenomenon as self-hating Jews.

In studying the cultural revolution and its meaning, we come face to face with the amazing stuck-in-timeness of the establishment left. They re-enact the same ceremonies of communal confession they invented in the 1960s (*Woe unto us for we are bigots!*), even while blacks rocket forward if they choose to, and girls swamp boys in grade school performance and college attendance, and the establishment at large strains every nerve (like a sailing ship with every rope creaking-tight) to favor blacks and other officially deserving minorities, along with women and other officially deserving majorities, over white males who were born *a full generation* after affirmative action became the taken-for-granted law of the land; white males who have never known a society that did not choose blacks and women over them. *White males*—what did they ever do anyway, aside from oppress people? *Huh?*

In contemplating our schools and colleges, we're struck by *their* bizarre stuck-in-timeness. The 1970s mood of relentless, this-is-good-for-you, take-your-medicine-and-shut-up disillusionment now thoroughly permeates teaching and textbook writing; in fact, much of book writing at large. I recently looked at a new guide to Paris that begins by soberly cautioning tourists that Paris is exciting and all that, but has passed through its periods of starvation, war and pestilence too! (So? . . . so . . . for God's sake *wipe that smile off your face* as you walk through the Tuileries! No joking around!)

The problem, of course, is that today's students were never illusioned to begin with; so their Disillusionment Training starts at o and works downward. Neither they nor most of their teachers have ever heard anything *good* about Western civilization, America, Judaism, Christianity, whites, males. Evidently the idea of a free nation, of a *just* nation trying always to be better, of a tolerant and generous nation, of Western science and mathematics, and medicine, and engineering, and the thirst for discovery, and Western painting and sculpture and architecture and music and literature—it all just happened, somehow or other. Obviously, young people haven't got any preconceptions in favor of America or WASPs or white males; *where on earth would they have got them?* Movies, books, TV and parts of the cybersphere all peddle the same shame-on-America nonsense fresh from 1967.

The new establishment is irritated by democracy, but that's not our biggest problem. The biggest: in the very largest sense, the PORGIs have missed the boat and missed the point. They are post-religious: atheist, agnostic or nothing-headed. They find themselves unable to believe in the God of the Jews or the God of the Christians—after (of course) sustained spiritual struggle and hard-fought encounters with the religion of their forefathers. They fail to see that faith in God is the keystone of two crossed arches, those two soaring arches at right angles that shelter Western civilization beneath the great span of a dramatic roof. Whether you believe in the keystone, or even know it is there, doesn't matter to the shelter itself. It doesn't matter if you loathe or don't understand theological engineering; the arches remain, and the shelter stands.

The space underneath the arches, in which every move you make and word you speak has moral echoes—that space *is* Western civilization. PORGIs would rather romp with their children outside among the buttercups and leave that high, grave, echoey space called Judeo-Christianity behind. (In fact, Jewish and Christian ethics differ in important ways, but emerge from the same two verses in the Hebrew Bible, the ones Jesus himself cites as the basis of his own faith: Luke 10:26–27.)

We understand that Christianity and Judaism are mere antiquated folk-nonsense to modern PORGIs, to the Porgiate generally—but then *why* and *how* should their children be good? Do PORGIs deploy some sort of complex neo-Kantian ethical framework in rearing their children? Where do young PORGIs go when they need answers to questions about right and wrong?

Or don't they ever ask those questions?

The nation's most serious problems are not economic or political. They are social, cultural, educational and (above all) spiritual. Conservative thinkers and leaders tend to ignore such problems. But our cultural oxygen is being displaced by a steady seep of poison. We had better act soon; in fact, now.

And we will. The problems are grave, but America has come through much worse.

It never hurts to remember that two of the gravest threats in American history happened within living memory. At the end of the 1920s our economy crumbled, and we suddenly passed from an age of plenty to an age of not enough, without having thought through the meaning of economic breakdown to modern democracy. And then the Japanese empire, having knifed us in the back on December 7, 1941, waged a ferocious, victorious war against this nation for half a year; beat us and threw us back again and again until American intelligence, brilliant naval risk taking and the heroism of two small groups of young men on torpedo planes and dive bombers turned the massive turret of history right around at Midway in June 1942. The sheer conviction with which they fought and died reminds us: it used to be said that America never lost a war. But the truth today, post–cultural revolution, is that America never lost a war unless it wanted to.

We have been in bad trouble and come through before. We will do it again—and if need be, again and again and again.

God bless this brave, proud, strong, wise, reckless and sublime nation, and its simple creed of liberty, equality, democracy, and its trust in American Zionism, America the shining city on a hill; and thank God for its history, its heroes, its each and every citizen, its admirers all over the world.

We have barely begun to bloom.

Woodbridge, 2012

Notes

PROLOGUE—BEFORE AND AFTER

1. Emily Post (Mrs. Price Post), *Etiquette* (New York and London: Funk & Wagnalls, 1940), p. 37.
2. Andrew Ferguson, "Press Man," *Commentary*, April 2011.
3. David Gelernter, *1939: The Lost World of the Fair* (New York: Free Press, 1995), p. 11.

CHAPTER 1—INTELLECTUALS AND THE CULTURAL REVOLUTION

1. William Clyde DeVane, *The American University in the Twentieth Century* (Baton Rouge: Louisiana State University Press, 1957), p. 22.
2. E. B. White, "Letter from the East," in *Essays of E. B. White* (New York: Harper & Row, 1979).
3. E. B. White, *Writings from the New Yorker: 1927–1976*, edited by Rebecca M. Dale (New York: HarperCollins, 1990), July 5, 1976.
4. Cited in Edmund Wilson, *The Sixties: The Last Journal, 1960–1972*, edited with an introduction by Lewis Dabney (New York: Farrar, Straus & Giroux, 1993), p. 78.

5. W. H. Auden, *The Dyer's Hand, and Other Essays* (New York: Random House, 1962), p. 319.

6. Norman Podhoretz, *Ex-Friends: Falling Out with Allen Ginsberg, Lionel and Diana Trilling, Lillian Hellman, Hannah Arendt, and Norman Mailer* (New York: Free Press, 1999), p. 187.

7. Norman Mailer, "The White Negro," in *Advertisements for Myself* (New York: G. P. Putnam, 1959), pp. 337–58.

8. Cited in Lionel Trilling, "George Orwell and the Politics of Truth," in *The Moral Obligation to Be Intelligent: Selected Essays,* edited and with an introduction by Leon Wieseltier (New York: Farrar, Straus & Giroux, 2000), p. 270.

9. George Orwell, "The Lion and the Unicorn: Socialism and the English Genius," in *Essays* (New York: Knopf, Everyman's Library, 2002), p. 300.

10. James Q. Wilson, "Justice versus Humanity in the Family," in *The Neoconservative Imagination: Essays in Honor of Irving Kristol,* edited by Christopher DeMuth and William Kristol (Washington, D.C.: AEI Press, 1995), p. 147.

11. Mary McCarthy, *Intellectual Memoirs: New York, 1936–1938* (New York: Harcourt Brace Jovanovich, 1992).

12. Cited in Paul Johnson, *Intellectuals* (London: Weidenfeld & Nicolson, 1988), p. 254.

13. Cited in Hannah Arendt, *Men in Dark Times* (New York: Harcourt, Brace & World, 1968), p. 188.

14. Mary McCarthy, *How I Grew* (San Diego: Harcourt Brace Jovanovich, 1987), p. 39.

15. Julien Benda, *The Treason of the Intellectuals* (1928), translated by Richard Aldington (New Brunswick, N.J.: Transaction Publishers, 2007).

16. Johnson, *Intellectuals,* p. 258.

17. Lionel Trilling, "George Orwell and the Politics of Truth," p. 270.

18. Nicola Chiaromonte, "The Student Revolt," in *The Worm of Consciousness and Other Essays,* edited by Miriam Chiaromonte (New York: Harcourt Brace Jovanovich, 1976).

19. Johnson, *Intellectuals,* p. 252.

20. Ibid., p. 260.

21. Thomas Hardy, *Jude the Obscure,* New Wessex Edition (London: Macmillan, 1974), p. 323.

22. Christopher Brooke, Roger Highfield, Wim Swaan, *Oxford and Cambridge* (New York: Cambridge University Press, 1988), p. 284.

23. Irving Kristol, *Reflections of a Neoconservative: Looking Back, Looking Ahead* (New York: Basic Books, 1983), p. 32.

24. *Between Friends: The Correspondence of Hannah Arendt and Mary McCarthy, 1949–1975,* edited and with an introduction by Carol Brightman (New York: Harcourt Brace, 1995), p. 230.

25. Hannah Arendt, "Lying in Politics," in *Crises of the Republic: Lying in Politics; Civil Disobedience; On Violence; Thoughts on Politics and Revolution* (New York: Harcourt Brace Jovanovich, 1972), p. 12.

26. Austin Bramwell, "The Revolt against the Establishment," introduction to William F. Buckley Jr., *God and Man at Yale: The Superstitions of "Academic Freedom"* (Washington, D.C.: Regnery, 2002), p. xvi.

27. DeVane, *The American University in the Twentieth Century,* p. 12 (see n. 1 above).

CHAPTER 2—SNAPSHOT 1941: WAR, THE ELITE AND THE THINKERS

1. *Life Magazine,* November 11, 1940, p. 34.

2. Diana Trilling, *The Beginning of the Journey: The Marriage of Diana and Lionel Trilling* (New York: Harcourt Brace, 1993).

3. Norman Podhoretz, *Breaking Ranks: A Political Memoir* (New York: Harper & Row, 1979), p. 176.

4. Irving Kristol, *Reflections of a Neoconservative: Looking Back, Looking Ahead* (New York: Basic Books, 1983), p. 12.
5. Cynthia Ozick, *Metaphor and Memory: Essays* (New York: Knopf, 1989), p. 114.
6. Diana Trilling, *The Beginning of the Journey*, p. 311.
7. Norman Mailer, *The Armies of the Night: History as a Novel, the Novel as History* (New York: New American Library, 1968), p. 112.
8. T. S. Eliot, "The Idea of a Christian Society," in *Christianity and Culture: The Idea of a Christian Society and Notes Toward the Definition of Culture* (New York: Harcourt Brace Jovanovich, 1968), p. 10.
9. George Orwell, "The Lion and the Unicorn: England Your England," in *Essays* (New York: Knopf, Everyman's Library, 2002), p. 295.
10. Nicola Chiaromonte, "The Student Revolt," in *The Worm of Consciousness and Other Essays,* edited by Miriam Chiaromonte (New York: Harcourt Brace Jovanovich, 1976), p. 60.
11. Cited in W. H. Auden, "The American Scene," in *The Dyer's Hand, and Other Essays* (New York: Random House, 1962), p. 322.

CHAPTER 3—THE GREAT REFORM
1. Cited in Leon Edel's introduction to Edmund Wilson, *The Twenties: From Notebooks and Diaries of the Period,* edited by Leon Edel (New York: Farrar, Straus & Giroux, 1975), p. xxix.
2. George P. Schmidt, *The Liberal Arts College: A Chapter in American Cultural History* (New Brunswick, N.J.: Rutgers University Press, 1957), p. 191.
3. Leon Edel, introduction to Edmund Wilson, *The Twenties*, p. xxix.
4. F. Scott Fitzgerald, *This Side of Paradise*, in *Novels and Stories, 1920–1922* (New York: Library of America, 2000), p. 34.
5. Alice Payne Hackett, *Wellesley: Part of the American Story* (New York: E. P. Dutton, 1949), p. 251.

6. Edmund Wilson, *The Sixties: The Last Journal, 1960–1972*, edited with an introduction by Lewis Dabney (New York: Farrar, Straus & Giroux, 1993), p. 25.

7. Ernest Havemann and Patricia Salter West, *They Went to College: The College Graduate in America Today* (New York: Harcourt Brace, 1952), p. 178.

8. Schmidt, *The Liberal Arts College*, p. 137.

9. Mary McCarthy, *The Group* (New York: Harcourt, Brace & World, 1963).

10. Irving Kristol, *Reflections of a Neoconservative: Looking Back, Looking Ahead* (New York: Basic Books, 1983), p. 6.

11. Randall Jarrell, *Pictures from an Institution* (New York: Knopf, 1954).

12. Mary McCarthy, *Intellectual Memoirs: New York, 1936–1938* (New York: Harcourt Brace Jovanovich, 1992), p. 65.

13. Norman Podhoretz, *Making It* (New York: Random House, 1967), p. 46.

14. F. Scott Fitzgerald, "Bernice Bobs Her Hair," in *Novels and Stories, 1920–1922*, p. 357.

15. Sinclair Lewis, "Young Man Axelbrod," in *Selected Short Stories of Sinclair Lewis* (New York: The Literary Guild, 1935), p. 285.

16. Tom Wolfe, *Radical Chic & Mau-Mauing the Flak Catchers* (New York: Farrar, Straus & Giroux, 1970), p. 29.

17. Wilson, *The Twenties*, p. 18.

18. Mary McCarthy, "Portrait of the Intellectual as a Yale Man," in *The Company She Keeps* (New York: Harcourt Brace, 1942), p. 169.

19. Fitzgerald, "Bernice Bobs Her Hair," in *Novels and Stories*, p. 357.

20. Schmidt, *The Liberal Arts College*, p. 201.

21. Fitzgerald, *This Side of Paradise*, in *Novels and Stories*, p. 65.

22. Fitzgerald, "Head and Shoulders," in *Novels and Stories*, p. 310.

23. Cited in Podhoretz, *Making It,* p. 46.

24. Mary McCarthy, *The Groves of Academe* (New York: Harcourt Brace, 1952), p. 139.

25. W. H. Auden, *The Dyer's Hand, and Other Essays* (New York: Random House, 1962), p. 320.

26. Norman Podhoretz, *Breaking Ranks: A Political Memoir* (New York: Harper & Row, 1979), p. 145.

27. McCarthy, *Intellectual Memoirs,* p. 22.

28. Mary McCarthy, *How I Grew* (San Diego: Harcourt Brace Jovanovich, 1987), p. 36.

29. Podhoretz, *Breaking Ranks,* p. 41.

30. Philip Roth, *The Facts: A Novelist's Autobiography* (New York: Farrar, Straus & Giroux, 1988), p. 90.

31. Jerome Karabel, *The Chosen: The Hidden History of Admission and Exclusion at Harvard, Yale, and Princeton* (Boston: Houghton Mifflin, 2005), p. 226.

32. Cited in Sandra Shoiock Roff, Anthony M. Cucchiara, Barbara J. Dunlap, *From the Free Academy to CUNY: Illustrating Public Higher Education in New York City, 1847–1997* (New York: Fordham University Press, 2000).

33. Irving Kristol, *Neoconservatism: The Autobiography of an Idea* (New York: Free Press, 1995), p. 469.

34. Lionel Trilling, *The Liberal Imagination: Essays on Literature and Society* (New York: Doubleday Anchor, 1950), p. vii.

35. Austin Bramwell, "The Revolt against the Establishment," introduction to William F. Buckley Jr., *God and Man at Yale: The Superstitions of "Academic Freedom"* (Washington, D.C.: Regnery, 2002), p. xii.

36. David Halberstam, *The Best and the Brightest* (New York: Random House, 1972), p. 220.

37. Podhoretz, *Making It,* p. 42.

38. Wolfe, *Radical Chic,* p. 83.

39. Cynthia Ozick, "Previsions of the Demise of the Dancing Dog," "Literature and the Politics of Sex: A Dissent" and

"Justice to Feminism," in *Art and Ardor: Essays* (New York: Knopf, 1983), pp. 263, 284, 261.

40. Wilson, *The Sixties*, p. 440.

41. Norman Mailer, *Miami and the Siege of Chicago: An Informal History of the Republican and Democratic Conventions of 1968* (New York: World Publishing Co., 1968), p. 35.

CHAPTER 4—IMPERIAL ACADEMIA

1. George P. Schmidt, *The Liberal Arts College: A Chapter in American Cultural History* (New Brunswick, N.J.: Rutgers University Press, 1957), p. 230.

2. Jacques Barzun, *The American University: How It Runs, Where It Is Going* (New York: Harper & Row, 1968), p. 12.

3. Mary McCarthy, "The Man in the Brooks Brothers Shirt," in *The Company She Keeps* (New York: Harcourt Brace, 1942), p. 123.

4. Mary McCarthy, *The Group* (New York: Harcourt Brace & World, 1963), p. 2.

CHAPTER 5—THE ROAD TO THE LATE '60S

1. Anatole Broyard, *Kafka Was the Rage: A Greenwich Village Memoir* (New York: Vintage Books, 1997), p. 8.

2. Randall Jarrell, *Pictures from an Institution* (New York: Knopf, 1954).

3. Norman Podhoretz, *Making It* (New York: Random House, 1967), p. 125.

4. Edmund Wilson, *The Sixties: The Last Journal, 1960–1972*, edited with an introduction by Lewis Dabney (New York: Farrar, Straus & Giroux, 1993), p. 537.

5. James Patterson, *Grand Expectations: The United States, 1945–1974* (New York: Oxford University Press, 1996), pp. 525–26.

6. *Between Friends: The Correspondence of Hannah Arendt and Mary McCarthy, 1949–1975*, edited and with an introduc-

tion by Carol Brightman (New York: Harcourt Brace, 1995), p. 181.

7. Norman Podhoretz, *Breaking Ranks: A Political Memoir* (New York: Harper & Row, 1979), p. 244.

8. *Between Friends: The Correspondence of Hannah Arendt and Mary McCarthy*, p. 181.

CHAPTER 6—SNAPSHOT 1968: WAR, THE ELITE AND THE THINKERS

1. Norman Mailer, *The Armies of the Night: History as a Novel, the Novel as History* (New York: New American Library, 1968), pp. 116ff.

2. Samuel G. Freedman, *The Inheritance: How Three Families and America Moved from Roosevelt to Reagan and Beyond* (New York: Simon & Schuster, 1996), pp. 316ff.

3. Christian G. Appy, *Working-Class War: American Combat Soldiers and Vietnam* (Chapel Hill: University of North Carolina Press, 1993).

4. George Steiner, *In Bluebeard's Castle: Some Notes Towards the Redefinition of Culture* (New Haven: Yale University Press, 1971), p. 115.

5. William J. Bennett, *The De-Valuing of America* (New York: Simon & Schuster, 1992), p. 175.

CHAPTER 7—TODAY: AIRHEADS AND OBAMACRATS

1. George Orwell, "Looking Back on the Spanish Civil War," in *Essays* (New York: Knopf, Everyman's Library, 2002), p. 439.

2. Hannah Arendt, "Lying in Politics," in *Crises of the Republic: Lying in Politics; Civil Disobedience; On Violence; Thoughts on Politics and Revolution* (New York, Harcourt Brace Jovanovich, 1972).

3. George Orwell, "Preface to the Ukrainian Edition of *Animal Farm*," in *Essays*, p. 1212.

4. Lionel Trilling, "George Orwell and the Politics of Truth," in *The Moral Obligation to Be Intelligent: Selected Essays*, edited

and with an introduction by Leon Wieseltier (New York: Farrar, Straus & Giroux, 2000), p. 274.

5. Ari L. Goldman, "Telling It Like It Wasn't," *Jewish Week*, August 9, 2011.

6. Arthur Herman, "The Gitmo Myth and the Torture Canard," *Commentary*, June 2009.

7. Joel Achenbach, "Final NASA shuttle mission clouded by rancor," *Washington Post*, July 1, 2011.

CHAPTER 8—ASYMMETRY AND BALANCE

1. Cited in Doro Bush Koch, *My Father, My President: A Personal Account of the Life of George H. W. Bush* (New York: Warner Books, 2006), p. 218.

2. Peter Wehner, "Obama, a 'Sort of God'?" Contentions, *Commentary Magazine* blog, June 8, 2009.

3. Michael Walsh, "The Turncoats," review of *Treason of the Heart* by David Pryce-Jones, *National Review*, June 20, 2011, p. 48.

CHAPTER 9—THE CULTURAL REVOLUTION SHAPES AMERICA

1. Norman Podhoretz, *Breaking Ranks: A Political Memoir* (New York: Harper & Row, 1979), p. 361.

2. Mary McCarthy, *The Groves of Academe* (New York: Harcourt Brace, 1952), p. 66.

3. Marcel Proust, *Remembrance of Things Past* [*A la recherche du temps perdu*], vol. I, translated by C. K. Scott Moncrieff and Terence Kilmartin (New York: Random House, 1981), p. 822.

4. Marcella Bombardieri and Maria Sacchetti, "Summers to step down, ending tumult at Harvard," *Boston Globe*, February 22, 2006.

5. Martin Amis, *The Moronic Inferno, and Other Visits to America* (London: J. Cape, 1986), p. 140.

6. Julian Young, *Friedrich Nietzsche: A Philosophical Biography* (New York: Cambridge University Press, 2010).

7. W. H. Auden, "The American Scene," in *The Dyer's Hand, and Other Essays* (New York: Random House, 1962), p. 321.

8. Kay S. Hymowitz, "Anti-Social Studies," *Weekly Standard,* May 6, 2002.

Index

McCarthy, Mary, 15; *The Group*, 42, 80, 132; *The Groves of Academe*, 140; on intellectuals' disputes, 11, 52; "The Man in the Brooks Brothers Shirt," 79, 119–20; and *Partisan Review*, 31; "Portrait of the Intellectual as a Yale Man," 45, 100; and Rahv, 11, 43; as "woman of letters," 19
McEwan, Ian, 114
McGovern, George, 102
McNamara, Robert, 25, 60–61, 86
Meacham, Jon, 126
medical science, 70–72; social status of, 82–83
Miami and the Siege of Chicago (Mailer), 74–75
Microbe Hunters (de Kruif), 70–71
Miller, Henry, 31
Miranda rights, 144
Mister Roberts (film), 83–84
Mohammed, Khalid Sheikh, 116–17
Molotov cocktail, 94–95
Monkey Business (film), 70
Monroe, Marilyn, 90
Moore, Mary Tyler, 85–87
Moses, Robert, 5
Mount Holyoke College, 42
MSNBC, 128, 129
Murrow, Edward R., 82

NASA, 70, 118–19
National Council for Social Studies, 151–52
National Guard, 104
National Public Radio, 126
"Nation at Risk, A," 108
Nazis, 1; and American Communists, 30; and bigotry exposed, 68–69; *Partisan Review* on, 31–32; and religion, 35; and Tea Party comparison, 126
NBC, 143
neoconservatism, 56, 91
New Haven: and illegal aliens, 143; and Rackley murder, 103–5; Schubert Theater, 41
New Left, 9, 23–24
Newsweek, 126; on Obama, 128
New Yorker, 29, 82
New York Herald Tribune, 5
New York Review of Books, 94–95
New York Times, 5, 102, 126; on Crown Heights riots, 112–13; on Obama, 127
1939: The Lost World of the Fair (Gelernter), 5
Nixon, Richard, 89; and affirmative action, 65, 132; as antiglamorous, 72; and Chicago convention, 74; education of, 87; and McGovern, 102; as tragic, 94; and Vietnam, 22